Penguin Books

The English Marriage

Drusilla Beyfus is married to Milton Shulman, the critic
and author, and they have three children. She lives in a
crowded flat in Eaton Square and during the school
holidays spends her time in the country. She has managed
to combine with marriage and parenthood a career as a
journalist, author and broadcaster. She is an Associate
Editor of the *Daily Telegraph Magazine*. Her book,
Lady Behave, written with Anne Edwards, has been accepted
as the standard work on modern etiquette. A well-known
television personality, she has appeared in such popular
programmes as 'Twenty Questions', 'First Impressions'
and 'Call My Bluff'. In whatever spare time she has,
she enjoys cooking, other people's gardens, modern
art exhibitions and contemporary design.

Drusilla Beyfus

The English Marriage

*What it is like to be
married today*

Penguin Books

Penguin Books Ltd, Harmondsworth,
Middlesex, England
Penguin Books Australia Ltd, Ringwood,
Victoria, Australia

First published by Weidenfeld & Nicolson 1968
Published in Penguin Books 1971
Copyright © Drusilla Beyfus, 1968

Made and printed in Great Britain by
C. Nicholls & Company Ltd
Set in Monotype Garamond

For my mother and father

Contents

Acknowledgements

I would like to thank all my interviewees for so
generously giving me their time and help, for submitting
to the rigours of being cross-questioned on the subject
of their own marriage, and for giving me permission
to publish the interviews. I would also like to thank,
Sally Williams, whose invaluable assistance in inter-
viewing a number of married people on my behalf gave
me more time for editing, and John Anstey, Editor of
the *Daily Telegraph Magazine*, for his unfailing
encouragement throughout the whole extended venture.
Finally, I must acknowledge the moral support of my
husband, who with a most uncharacteristic display of
patience has listened to my obsessive going-on about
this book for nearly three years.

Foreword

This book largely originated in my curiosity about the extra-ordinary human condition known as being married. I used to look at my married friends and acquaintances and wonder if they felt, as I did, a peculiar awareness of the married state. For whatever else may or may not be said about marriage, the feeling of being a married person is totally and absolutely unlike the consciousness of being single.

The specific situation of marriage between individuals creates of its own volition elusive and complex relationships. The conflicts, the rewards, the phases, the dramas and bore-doms of married life tend to make fiction seem pallid in com-parison with the actuality of marriage – if only the truth were known. The world of men and women in marriage is a sub-terranean universe fed by hidden motivational streams. People behind their married screens have personalities quite different from those they usually reveal to their relatives, friends and acquaintances. Perhaps, in order to know a person really well, you have to marry them.

Maybe it was this, to me, impenetrably private nature of marriage that first stimulated the idea of attempting to portray some of its qualities and characteristics in this book.

In addition to my fascination with the nature of the marital tie, I was also conscious of the fact that marriage was changing. New situations, new demands, new problems were emerging out of the differently ordered society in which we live in this country. One of the major changes in attitudes towards marriage is that society no longer exerts a traditional pressure on married couples to stay together – marriage is now a much more personal and voluntary affair and as such is much more interesting.

What I have tried to do is to produce some evidence – in terms of other people's married lives – which creates an impression of what it is like to be married today. I have concentrated principally on marriages which are still valid, on one level or another, as far as the husbands and wives involved are concerned. With two exceptions I have not attempted to express the problems arising out of formal separation or divorce because this stage marks the end of the married relationship. I selected the couples whom I interviewed on the basis that their married lives were of interest in their own right, and also that some aspect of their marriage struck a contemporary note. In some cases, I interviewed the husband or the wife only. This was because the other partner was not available to see me at the time, or they felt that they had little to add to the comments of their partner.

The method by which I obtained most of my material was to tape-record a long informal conversation between myself and the person interviewed. Generally I preferred to see husbands and wives separately, as I felt it was easier for them to talk freely on their own. As a general rule we talked for several hours discussing their married lives in the round rather than concentrating on a single aspect or problem. Once the tapes were transcribed, I set about editing the questionnaires into the form in which they are published here.

In a minority of cases, the people whom I interviewed have permitted me to publish their real names. But in those instances where husbands and wives have naturally wished to protect their identity, I have changed names, the area they live in, occupations and other details, although every attempt has been made to retain the significance and atmosphere of the original situation.

Reactions to the experience of being interviewed on marriage varied according to the individuals, but I noticed a general distinction between the sexes. Wives I found to be almost obsessively interested both in their own marriage and in the dilemmas common to all married couples. Men tended to be bored with the idea of discussing the minutiae of married life and to wonder who on earth would be interested in it. But amongst younger husbands and wives too I found an increased awareness of themselves in relation to the state of being married. Older married couples tended to accept matrimony as part of the air they breathed, not to think about it particularly. The young people adopted a more introspective approach in which they analysed their own reactions, emotions and feelings towards the marital tie.

The accounts of married life which emerged from my interviews provide some personal clues to the answers to such questions as, 'how do married couples cope, react, adjust to changing social conditions?' – 'what is happening to the institution of marriage in this country?' – 'what does it feel like to be married now?' – 'what effect have children on a marriage?' The contemporary mood is stressed because in so many ways marriage has been reshaped by the shifting patterns of English society. So much is new, and in common with many other institutions marriage has had to undergo adjustments in its values and attitudes.

The causes of social change are many-sided and various, but amongst the influences which have directly impinged on the character of marriage must be counted the breakdown of class barriers, the decline of parental influence, the spread of affluence, the growing permissiveness of social attitudes, particularly in relation to sex and morals, and the retreating hold of religion. I would also mention, in the category of major sources of change in this field, the increased earning power of women, the replacement of the old-fashioned extended family group by smaller households and the ever-widening spread of the influence of the State in its welfare and educational services.

I found that some marriages have been radically changed by the ways in which the partners have responded to the new challenges. Others, and I dare say the majority, have been touched only marginally by specifically modern conditions. These relationships would have much in common with their parents' and grandparents', and it is not with these that I am primarily concerned in this book. However, the existence of what might be called an old-fashioned marriage is represented here.

1. *The need to be free*

Alexander and Rosie

The Situation. A young couple attempt to work out a personal code of values in a marriage which is shaped by drug taking, mysticism and a marked mood of opting out. The pair have been married for two years.

The Husband. Alexander, aged twenty-three. He is long-haired, dresses as an exquisite, and his family is listed in Burke's *Landed Gentry*. He is a public-school boy who works on the fringe of the film world.

The Wife. Rosie, aged twenty-four. She is the daughter of working-class parents and left secondary modern school at fifteen to work in a dress shop. She does occasional paid jobs, mostly modelling for fashion photography or helping out friends who run bistros or boutiques.

The Place. One room in a large communal flat off the King's Road, Chelsea, shared by several friends. The bedsitting room is imaginatively furnished in psychedelic-pop vein.

ALEXANDER: Rosie looks like a Botticelli, she is like his Venus except that her hair is darker. I stole her from my best friend. I just looked at her, and I could see that there was nothing else.

ROSIE: I thought he was beautiful, but he was a bit of a beatnik then, rather scruffy.

We went off to Bournemouth to live together. It was rather strange and it didn't really work. I wasn't ready to live with him. I had told my parents that I was going away for a holiday beside the sea, and I felt guilty because I knew they wouldn't approve.

ALEXANDER: She wasn't keen on the idea of living with me outside of marriage because her parents thought she was a virgin. She didn't bribe me into getting married. She said, 'Let's get married,' and I decided not to say no, in about two telephone calls.

I realized that Rosie has not got a lot of knowledge but she has a fantastic imagination and she is very intuitive, and that was what I was specially knocked out about in her. Her taste in clothes, her sense of selection was fantastic. She is a great guide to my own taste.

ROSIE: Several times we were going to get married and I couldn't go through with it. I had to tell him. The prospect made me feel weird, I couldn't sleep and felt extraordinary.

Then suddenly I decided I did want to marry him.

ALEXANDER: My father didn't want me to get married. He said to me, 'Don't marry a stupid woman, your mother has a little mind.' He married my mother, and I'm very close to her, when he was up at Oxford and she was a local working girl and he thought my situation was comparable. My parents are divorced, and my father's second marriage is a nothing. I may do some strange things, but face to face with your wife in court? Freak me out.

My father, between him and me, it's very strange. I feel fantastically affectionate towards the idea of a father but when we do meet we don't connect, there's no communication. He used to find my clothes absolutely repellent. He was convinced that long hair meant dirt and madness, and then he found out that I wasn't dirty or mad.

But he didn't like Rosie and he didn't come to our wedding.

ROSIE: I was frightened of Alexander's father. The one time I went to his house I fell asleep on his bed immediately.

He is very, very shy of Alexander because he left him when he was young and they don't really know one another. It's odd being with them, they are so distant. It's not like father and son.

He probably didn't think I was good enough for Alexander, or something.

ALEXANDER: I put on a grey suit and a shirt and tie and we got married in a Registry Office. I felt awful for two days afterwards. But after a while it makes no difference whether you are married or not, except to other people. The bond is outside the realm of words.

ROSIE: My Mum and Dad came to the wedding but they were worried. Alexander didn't have a job and they thought perhaps he would never get a proper job.

After the wedding, I felt really awful. We had a huge party of Alexander's friends and I was scared of everybody. I've always been like that, I feel an outsider.

I felt as if I had been put in a cage. I was unhappy for about a fortnight and then I became very happy. We had about twenty pounds saved up between us and he had his grant and we lived in one room.

ALEXANDER: When I'm with her I don't have to worry if I feel bad, uncomfortable or not at ease. I can tell her and the fact doesn't sweep her into being afraid as well.

ROSIE: I love Alexander and I don't think I shall stop. I give him love, look after him, cook his meals, do his washing and hope he likes me.

Probably, he needs someone more intelligent than I am. I wish I could understand things more. I'm fairly perceptive, but I find it difficult to read some of his books. I used to worry, but now I think that loving each other is more important.

ALEXANDER: When we are together at home we go back into our childhood and behave as half the time we truly want to behave. We play children's games. On the spur of the moment we make up words for objects in our room. The game is whether the other person is able to guess or deduce what the actual object is. We might call a book-end a crane, the person who is guessing has to share the same thought-process as the namer. We almost have the same idea-associations, which is incredible considering how big the Kingdom is.

ROSIE: Most evenings we stay at home listening to music, and smoking pot. I don't smoke as much as he does. He gets quite hung-up if he doesn't have any. He's all right, but he likes the state of being stoned. I find it makes me feel very good, but lazy. As I like to have everything tidy I do the work first.

ALEXANDER: Smoking pot sharpens my mind, takes the unnecessary tensions out of my mind and relieves me of the pettiness of various irritations. I disapprove of drinking alcohol. Drink does not refine, and makes people stupid.

I have smoked pot since I was seventeen and I get psychologically hung-up if I know there is none to smoke at home. Rosie can't do anything when she smokes, so if she has a lot of ironing or washing she doesn't smoke. But I go to work on pot.

ROSIE: When I take a trip I like to have somebody near that I really know and love. Really it is an experience you should have on your own.

LSD has an incredible effect. We lie down on the bed and go. I close my eyes and have wonderful visions – like going into Wonderland. I see incredible lakes and strange Indian people gliding down a river in a boat in colours that are there all the time but which you don't normally see.

When I read a book or look at a painting I get right into the work. It is like looking into an artist's mind.

The experience is very beautiful, very rich and full but it can get out of hand. I have suffered on it. LSD is such a truth drug. I have been outside on it sometimes, but that is very disturbing because when you look at the people out there they look so terrible some of them, they look so sad. If you go on a tube most people seem to be sort of paranoid, they seem to suffer and it is really quite horrific for me.

Gradually, after eight hours we come down. I am usually very tired as I use up so much energy.

The legal aspect of taking LSD is a frightening thing, it

does worry me. I've never seen a policeman when I've been on LSD. I might be able to handle the situation very well, but maybe I couldn't. It would depend on how high I was.

ALEXANDER: We have had incredible ups and downs with money. I don't bother with it. If I have it, I spend it or we spend it, if we don't have it then we try to get some. For what I do I should earn twice as much, but I don't bother to ask for a rise because I believe that you should work without view to reward. I let it all come to me as much as possible.

ROSIE: It's good to have an interest, to do something. Alexander is very interested in his work, but if he didn't have to earn money he would concentrate on studying. I don't mind if he doesn't make it in his world. I never think beyond today. If we are really short of money I can always pick up a bit by modelling, or making dresses.

ALEXANDER: She wants a baby more than anything. But she is waiting to find out how significant it is, what it is. We are both groping in the dark. I'm terribly scared to have a child, I wouldn't know what to tell it except, be kind. I would have to learn from the child.

ROSIE: I would like to have three children. I wouldn't work, I would devote my time to looking after them. I shall take my trips in the evening when the baby is asleep. People do take trips that have children.

I shall try to understand my child. Now, my mother couldn't really understand me. I was lonely when I was little. My sister was always the one that did everything good and I was always the naughty one. I was always doing things wrong and my parents couldn't understand why I rebelled. I was the pretty one when I was taken out, but in the family I was the naughty one. My mother did her best. She thought she was doing the right thing.

ALEXANDER: Intellectually I recognize that you are doomed if you think a person is yours. We can't possess anything. Possession is an illusion. But I find it frustrating because whereas it is clear to me that Rosie is not mine and she belongs to everybody I do suffer from jealousy. She has been whipped off once already. Fortunately, he was someone I had great respect for. In a way, I could have made it with him too. But, if she had produced a baby by him, I would have felt desperately unhappy.

ROSIE: Ideally, everybody should be able to make it with each other. But it doesn't really seem to work. I like to feel that Alexander is mine. I do. I get unhappy when I think of him sleeping with another girl because I think he might prefer her to me and might want to go off with her. It's just jealousy. Maybe I can get over this thing.

ALEXANDER: She found out that I was sleeping with someone else, and she had to accept the situation which was quite something because it wasn't even a woman. She blew her top completely, and she became very violent as she often does.

She broke through because the four of us – the boy with whom she was having this simple affair, and my friend – we all went and had dinner together and talked about it. My friend explained how it had happened between us and she had to look him in the eye. He was so cool about it that she and I could say, 'Look, we haven't lost anything over this.'

ROSIE: It hurt me. It mattered. I have a terrible temper and I had to get it over with. I hit Alexander and told him I wanted to kill him. He slapped my face, he has to do that to stop me from hitting him, and it does. He doesn't like hurting me, but he has to slap me because if not I get very hysterical.

I learnt a lot from my own affair. It just showed me I was happiest with Alexander. I found making love to Alexander and to someone else very confusing and disturbing. I did love my friend but it wasn't a very strong feeling. I don't think he is nearly such a nice person as Alexander – he was really very selfish. My affair began when we took LSD together.

I feel such incredible love when I take LSD. Probably now I won't take much more LSD, I don't have the urge to take it.

Everybody was telling me how beautiful the experience was and I wanted to try it. I am frightened of what LSD can do to me physically because they are finding out certain drawbacks about the drug.

ALEXANDER: I have tried heroin and cocaine, but apart from the fact that they do kill, the effect is not worth it. On LSD I hear a piece of music and become it, totally, and I work towards that on pot.

Pot does not act as an aphrodisiac, but if we do make it after we have smoked, sex is better. I can go easy, be leisurely, go into the sensation more, forget who I am or where I am. I stop thinking of myself as a separate entity and I become one with everything.

ROSIE: When you live together with somebody, you don't need that much sex, maybe once a week. When you have been together for so long, sex changes and becomes a very deep love. You become closer and live more as one person. I could rush around going with everybody but that would be silly.

I was brought up that sex was bad, wrong, and what changed my mind was having sex. But I would hate to sleep with someone I did not love.

I change from day to day. Sometimes I feel good, sometimes I feel frightened and like hiding in a corner. It always goes round in a circle.

I'm worried I might go mad. I feel I might go over the edge. I'm frightened of death more than anything, and I am scared of getting cancer. My young brother recently died of cancer.

Drugs have helped me a lot, so has the fact that I'm older. I just think that my friends are so much kinder, people are more understanding because most of my friends all take drugs and it has brought us all much closer. But then so many of my friends seem to be getting rather weird. I don't know if it's by taking LSD but they can't play the games any more. LSD takes you so far out that for some people it is more difficult to live in this society because you see what is wrong and you see what you should do. I think that you should try and be as loving as you can towards everybody and that is really rather difficult, it is so difficult to get along with people.

ALEXANDER: When I come into contact with another person, I don't want to say anything to anybody. We have a pitter-patter relationship – 'Hello, how are you?' Often, I don't even want to say, 'How are you?'

Between people, words are a hang-up. What matters is suddenly feeling divine. You get this great feeling of being alive when two people are together and the vibrations are mingling, just standing together and watching the sunrise.

It is easier to respond with someone you love, but you make the ultimate step alone.

Simon and Carey

The Situation. A sociable and informed young couple make a conscious attempt to preserve their individual identities within the context of lasting marriage. The couple have been married for five years and they have three children under four.

The Husband. Simon, in his late twenties, who comes from an upper-middle-class family. Educated at public school and Oxbridge, he gave up an academic career – he had been a Fellow at an American University – to follow his business interests.

The Wife. Carey, in her mid-twenties, was educated at private school and trained as a secretary. She has a private income.

The Place. A pretty, nineteenth-century terrace house with a small garden in Shepherd's Bush.

SIMON: She is a very, very pretty girl, and that was a good reason for wanting to marry her, for a start. She is also a very, very tough girl, in terms of being resilient, and courageous. I figured that if she was going to participate in the world I was likely to go on living in, she would have to have these qualities.

She is implacable and unforgiving and if someone has done something wrong, not necessarily towards me or the children, but towards one of her friends – if someone had said something untrue, and wrong and immoral she would be ruthlessly implacable in her attitude towards that person.

CAREY: When he said, 'Will you marry me?' I said 'Yes, sure', immediately. I was only too delighted. I thought, he knows so many girls, I had better get it in quick. He maintains he only married me because he got very drunk and proposed by accident which is not true. He was quite sober.

SIMON: We always pretend I was smashed – it's not true. I was in Mexico with her, and it wasn't a question of being smashed, it was the altitude. Mexico City is 8000–9000 feet, it's very unsettling. Many people have made terrible mistakes in Mexico!

CAREY: I thought I might have to sit it out for three or four years – I had been living with him in his flat for a year before we married. I was determined to marry him or be part of his life. It sounds tough but I was much happier with him and possibly he was with me too.

There's a compulsion on you to get married before you are twenty-five. I was twenty. There is so much enthusiasm for being young. At seventeen you feel that twenty-five is very old and the world will come to an end. Probably, at the age at which I married you could be married to a lot of people because you are in the early stages of your development. Marriage undoubtedly influences you strongly afterwards, especially in my case with Simon being such a strong character. I don't know whether he has been influenced by me at all, I shouldn't think so.

SIMON: I never felt the 'we' of marriage, never. I think of Carey as a person that I have been living with for five years. She is not called Mrs Simon Brown, she is called Carey Brown because that's who she is. When her friends write they write to her as Carey Brown. This is not imposed on her by me, or by herself or by anybody. I certainly do not call her darling myself. Darling is a hopeless word.

D. H. Lawrence discusses this 'we' fusion of identities living in close proximity. He uses wonderfully graphic images about helping your wife into her knickers. He's absolutely right. This was, and to a large extent still is, what marriage is all about – 'Will you come out to dinner tonight?' 'I'm not sure whether we can.' 'Yes, I'd love to, but I'm not sure whether Angela – well, hang on and I'll ask her.' Angela or whoever it is.

This is very dangerous and characterizes ninety per cent of the marriages I know, and is destructive totally of what is called a relationship, though I never know what this word relationship means. 'Have we got a good relationship?' 'Yes, marvellous, it's in the cupboard.'

De La Mare quotes a definition of love as being a condition in which two solitudes touch and hold and protect each other – an existence of two totally separate identities who can live together and on many levels complement each other. To illustrate the point crudely, I am a better shot than Carey, but she is a better cook than I am.

CAREY: I would be just as happy if I was unmarried and just living with him. Certainly I would be prepared to have his children. The fact that I am married makes life simpler – the neighbours, parents and everything else. I find there is very little difference between marriage and living together. What is nice about being married is what is nice about being with one particular man. It's great to be with and live with somebody you love. He's not remotely dull, he's one of the most – I'm probably biased – intelligent men I've ever met and an authority on a wide range of subjects he doesn't necessarily use at the moment.

He hates me defending him, but you always do if somebody is being rude about a friend. He gets attacked a lot, inevitably. People like him always do. A defence almost always involves an explanation and he never explains. What he does is to say to the person, well, you may be right, and this is how he wants me to react. Sometimes I do and sometimes I don't – it depends on how much I like or dislike the person who is criticizing him.

SIMON: I don't think she would support me if I was in the wrong – I doubt if I could count on her support. Her moral judgements are based on a code of values she has worked out for herself. She's got a good mind. She's good when she reads or looks at paintings and out of all this she gets a framework of reference which is pretty accurate.

If somebody has had a considerable academic training, as I have, there must be certain areas that are not shared by the person who has not had that experience. But I don't find a gulf. If there is something that she wants to talk about, or I want to talk about, it gets discussed. It's not a question of her being able to keep up, as that sounds competitive and I would never consider ourselves competitive.

CAREY: He is very highly charged – always doing things. During the day he runs his business and in the evenings he does his committee work, and later on his research work which goes on until about two o'clock in the morning.

In the evening when he works at home, I paint, or I sew or I watch telly. Sometimes I work at a table in his study, but it is in a place where I can't see him.

Children are one of the big things of his life. He is marvellous with children. Totally strange neurotic little children will come up who wouldn't go to anyone else and accept him straight.

I get terribly scared when I am going to have a kid. When I had our first baby he hung around the nursing home with half a bottle of scotch hanging out of his pocket, he just wandered in and out of my room. I don't believe he was there during the delivery – it is of no particular value for me to have Simon there. The only thing I do remember is my gynaecologist relaying information like a football commentary, which were the stages.

After the baby arrived, he used to turn up in the evenings at about seven-thirty, have a glass of scotch and wander away again. He didn't think of sending flowers. But for Charlotte, my new baby, I insisted he sent some for a party I had in my room on my last night in the hospital, and they came with a lovely little note saying 'Love from Simon' in someone else's handwriting.

The one drawback to marriage is being pregnant because it's rather like being ill and Simon does not understand. He says, 'Sweetheart, why don't you go to bed?' and I hang around saying, 'I feel awful, but I've got to do the washing-up.' He says, 'I'll do the washing-up', and I say, 'You don't understand, do you? It's not that I want you to do the washing-up.'

He doesn't help with practical things such as nappies because he doesn't have to. We have a nanny. At night when the new baby cries he digs me in the back and says, 'Baby is crying' and I climb out of bed and do it. I don't like sleeping with a tiny baby in the bedroom. I lie awake and listen to the grunting and wonder if I will have to get up for a feed.

To begin with I had a sixteen-year-old girl called Lucy who then became a deb and left. She was very good, not that she was trained or did all the right things. But she would take the baby out, and do anything that happened to need doing. She was not practical for baby-sitting because she used to go out a lot herself. I used to take my first baby everywhere. I tucked her under my arm and took her shopping and since I was breast-feeding I fed her in the most peculiar places – sitting in the changing-room at Waterloo station, places like that. When I went out to dinner with people I knew, I put her on their bed.

This generation has a totally changed attitude towards children, because even my parents adopted the viewpoint, 'Look what we have done for you, why aren't you grateful?'

Small babies are mostly all joy. You get this tiny human being who thinks you are God, who doesn't really demand anything much of you. Sometimes, obviously, babies get on your nerves because they want your time when you are busy, they want to be picked up and so on, but the important thing is that they totally accept you as you are.

SIMON: The pressures on Carey with three children under four – even given that we have a nurse – are such that the mechanics of living tend to take over, and our own interests get to be excluded. Piles of undone washing can rub and fray at a marriage, the whole boring apparatus of having to do washing and cooking breeds pressures, especially for people like ourselves who opt to have a lot of children because we like children. If a girl has a personality of her own with ideas of her own I think the frustrations of domestic chores can be frightening.

CAREY: The more involved you are with your children, the more likely you are to want to have more of them. Contraception is so good nowadays that having children is likely to be a conscious decision rather than a haphazard event. My age group and income group seem to be having a lot more children. It may be a reaction against the previous generation which was 'two' conscious. Simon's mother had two then two again simply because she remarried. My generation spends more time in the company of our children, much more. We either can't afford a house big enough to have resident help, or girls like myself who employ nannies – having been brought up by them ourselves – find that nannies, particularly the young ones, are very different these days. They have a lot more time off and want a life of their own.

I think that if you have a nanny you like your children an awful lot more. If you haven't got good help, and you have several children, inevitably there are masses of options you can't take up. For instance, Simon usually comes home at seven and says, 'We've been asked to go out to dinner with the So-and-so's', and I say, having no help, 'I can't', and then eventually you begin to resent it because it is your children who prevent you from enjoying a social life. In the early days of our marriage this happened time and time again. He would be out most evenings until two or three o'clock in the morning and I would be stuck in the flat with the baby. I could get a baby-sitter but what baby-sitter can you get who wants to stay until three in the morning? If I had known at five o'clock in the afternoon I could have at least found someone who would have enabled me to go out for a while, but again Simon's life is not like that. He tends much more to come back at seven saying 'we are going out'.

SIMON: Carey has an income from a trust fund. One day I guess she will be a very rich girl, she must be, I don't see how she can help it.

We have been very short of money. We figured, right, we are short. Something's got to go. What's it going to be? It may be a painting that I have bought that goes or it might be a brooch Carey was given by her grandparents.

I don't give her any money to run the house. Whoever is in funds at the time pays the bills. It is an utterly illogical method but it seems to work.

If the telephone bill arrives, and I'm away and Carey's got the money, she pays it, if not, she throws it at me when I come back and says can you deal with this? We don't have anything like a joint account but if we want to buy a thing, whoever has the cash buys it, and of course by and large it gets to be me because I earn a lot of money.

CAREY: Simon inherited some money from his parents, not a lot but enough to set him up. He makes a lot of money and loses a lot of money. He doesn't spend much on himself unless he is gambling on the horses.

SIMON: Before I married, I did experience being with somebody who was entirely dependent on me financially and it did affect us. If you live in a capitalist society everybody works out for themselves a certain style of living. You may be rich and choose an Up-the-Junction style of living, or you may be pressed for money and elect to dine at Wheeler's every night. When you haven't got enough money to support your style, when you suddenly run out of rope financially, this situation can be explosive – and can be a tremendous factor in breaking up a marriage.

CAREY: We have separate bank accounts, separate banks in fact. If he gets a big cheque in and I want some of it I ask him, and conversely. But we tend to know how much the other has in hand because we know when either one is good for a touch. Very much on that basis. If I see something I want, I tend to buy it anyway. I bring it back and say, 'Look, I couldn't live without it.'

Generally, we buy things for the house independently. I can tell which things in the drawing-room are mine and which are his. His new folly is a carved stone mantelpiece which he brought back yesterday. I wasn't sure if I did like it at first but now I've come round to it. It has to be fixed in.

SIMON: She has a different sense of humour to mine. What she thinks is extremely funny sometimes I don't. I think her sense of humour is Shakespearian in terms of forms like puns which sometimes I understand, mostly I don't. She has a very quick sense of humour in many directions. Sometimes I don't see it. But there's never been a collision over laughter.

CAREY: At home our fights tend to be about very small issues – we haven't developed any serious personal friction. Last night it was about whether I was tired. Simon kept saying, 'Go up and have a bath and come back when you feel better.' I merely sat in a chair saying, 'I feel ghastly, I feel dead.' It was one of those occasions when you take it out on the nearest moveable object. I was tired though. I had been spring-cleaning my cupboards.

He hates rows and I'm much better at them than he is.

SIMON: I spend about thirty to thirty-five per cent of the year out of the country, totally away. And there are other ways of being absent, to the extent that it is possible for me to go forty-eight hours virtually without being in contact with Carey. If I work late, I then go out possibly to play cards and I'll come back in the small hours and rise very early. So we can go two days without really communicating, although physically I've set eyes on her.

I have to go abroad a lot for my business, but sometimes I go for the ride, when there is no necessity for me to go. Last year I went to Africa on a zoological expedition, purely because I was fascinated by such an extraordinarily interesting world. I go away nearly every year for two or three weeks to my brother's house on the west coast of Scotland, and I live on my own up there.

Carey certainly needs her friends when I go away. But she probably has the opportunity to go out more frequently than when I am here. My friends are very fond of her and very possessive about her. They will telephone her immediately and say, 'Right, you can't stay in tonight, we are going to go and have dinner.'

She has admirers, certainly. There's one sweet one who is enormously rich and is always turning up and taking her out to lunch in a gigantic Bentley. He eyes me a bit warily when I come down the stairs and takes my fishing rod off to be repaired at Hardy's. She deals with him very abruptly, though I think she is fond of him.

When Carey married me she came across into another world and brought nobody with her. I won't have most of her family in the house so for her it was a considerable step, for this reason alone. Having been adopted by the people I like, she has that circle and there are others who come in.

As I am away so much, a consistent possibility is that she will meet someone else. But if that happened I would accept the situation fully. I would mind terribly if it happened, I can't conceive of the possibility, but if it did, I would know that it would not have worked.

CAREY: It would be nicer if Simon was here, or I was with Simon. I miss him and waiting is a hell of a long time, but it is perfectly possible. Last year Simon flew back to see me twice in the middle of his four-month away trip. I was on holiday in Italy for one reunion – the sun makes it worse when you are on your own. You get very randy.

I find that either of us can push the other one over to the other's mood, but it certainly takes a long time to adjust sexually. Sex does get better, absolutely. You might see an incredibly attractive man that you fancy very strongly and when it actually comes to the point it is not as good as it ought to be.

At home if he is out until four o'clock in the morning the odds are that he is getting smashed at his club but very unlikely that he is going to bed with a girl. He finds he likes talking to men more.

SIMON: It is marvellous, or has been in my experience, to screw somebody that you like or love. If it works, that's fine.

The need to prove or affirm my security by having affairs was an aspect of my earlier insecurity. Anybody who comes out of the bleak, sadistic, monastic background of the English upper classes and their education, and is alienated from it as hopelessly as I was, is liable to be insecure. So then one's whole first series of affairs is an affirmation of identity. What I think is marvellous that can happen after that stage is when you lay a bird and you are there the following morning and her breath smells bad and she looks terrible, and you can laugh and kiss her. Then the conquest thing is over and perhaps, if she can laugh too, you have had an encounter of value.

CAREY: I assume he loves me. After all, he married me and wants me to have his children, so I think that's enough demonstration for starters. Although, again, when you are pregnant you want continual reassurance and I am practically always pregnant.

SIMON: I have lived for five years with one girl and I've had three children with her and we've been through tempests in terms of what's happened. I don't get anything 'out' of it, the very phrase comes from *The Forsyte Saga* and it's a phrase from the capitalist world. I don't count any dividends. I have lived in strife and happiness with one girl.

I'm making no prognostications about the future. I don't see anything except that everything changes, but beyond that I have never thought of divorce or separation. I, and Carey in a different way, are very much stronger than most other people. It's as simple as that.

Andrew and Marianne Sinclair

The Situation. Both husband and wife attempt to evolve separate, independent identities within a highly personal concept of marriage. The couple have been married for six years.

The Husband. Andrew Sinclair, aged thirty-two, author and novelist.

The Wife. Marianne Sinclair, aged twenty-six. An exceptionally attractive girl. She is Parisian-born and has become a novelist writing in the English language.

The Place. Mrs Sinclair's flat in London.

MARIANNE SINCLAIR: I met Andrew at a party when I was nineteen and decided within ten minutes that I had met the first and probably the last man I would be happy married to. I announced to my mother that evening that if he asked me to marry him right away I would, even though I had no idea whether I was going to see him again.

ANDREW SINCLAIR: We married as total strangers, one always does. It was just one vast explosion of love between us. She corresponded to my myths and I corresponded to hers. She was always in love with Charles Laughton and I had an appalling melancholia and a type of face rather too large for my body. I always believed in very literary, very thin-boned girls, rather dry. We just made each other's myths clunk-clunk, and there you are. After a year or so I began to know her. Then I found we were totally unsuited to each other, but that didn't matter.

MARIANNE SINCLAIR: To begin with we lived in the closest possible circumstances, and this period was the only time in my life when I felt properly married. In fact when we moved into a four-room apartment I was completely lost at being one end of the flat and Andrew at the other. I would feel as if he had disappeared for ever and be compelled to rush into the room where he was.

ANDREW SINCLAIR: From the very beginning I tried to help Marianne to be independent, and today she doesn't need my help. By the time she was twenty-five she had her own career, her own flat, her own bank account. I didn't train her, she trained herself. What I did was say, 'All right, let's work on your having a career, I'll help you buy a flat of your own. I'll help to teach you how to run a bank account and all the idiotic details of life which mean you can manage on your own.' I suppose I was her university teacher too. I taught her history and the English language, obviously. I have been patriotic from the start and she writes her novels in English.

On her side she taught me everything I know about the psychology of women because I have never lived with a woman for six years before.

MARIANNE SINCLAIR: The great difference between Andrew and I when we got married was that Andrew had a whole life outside of me. He had a whole field of interests which were completely outside the sphere of marriage or a relationship with a woman. I had none of these things, so there was this fantastic inequality between us. If Andrew had not pushed me to develop some kind of outside interests, some kind of career, I would have had nothing.

ANDREW SINCLAIR: I always said from the beginning that I may need to be alone to write. We agreed on this, that you have to choose every day to remain with somebody. I am a writer first and a husband afterwards, I hope.

MARIANNE SINCLAIR: About a year ago Andrew decided to sacrifice our marriage, temporarily anyway, to a literary project. He needed to be alone to write a novel about obsessional loneliness. So we separated, and spent our time apart in our own flats. He has a place at Limehouse, and I have a London flat, and a small apartment in Paris. There are times when we meet about twice a week – we spend the evening and night together, or sometimes we are together for the weekend. He comes here or I go to him, or we meet in Paris.

I am never so fond of my husband as when we meet on these brief spells. It is like a honeymoon, or exactly like not being married again and we are back to those all too brief two or three months when we would desperately long to see each other the whole week and meet at weekends. I had forgotten the excitement I could feel at seeing Andrew again. And it wasn't that I had grown bored with him before that – we still enjoyed each other's company and conversations very much – but I had forgotten the emotion of being able to go from departures to meetings and backwards and forwards. It was lovely.

ANDREW SINCLAIR: You can't write drunk, you can't write on drugs but you can write on facts. You have got to be free to go where you want when you want. I couldn't do it if I was in the frame of mind where I was living a normal rational life with a woman.

MARIANNE SINCLAIR: I feel I shouldn't telephone him more than twice daily, which makes me feel brave about not disturbing him and interfering.

When we separated it was the first time I had been on my own, having gone directly from my mother's care to my husband. Suddenly I discovered the charm of being totally oneself, and living at one's own pace. When we come together it is true that I do begin to feel unhappy at the prospect of leaving each other again. I feel a kind of terror and no, I can't be alone again. But as soon as we are apart I feel happy again about being alone, and confident.

I think you can only do this if you feel very confident of the other person. Otherwise I would spend all the time he wasn't with me wondering if he wants me back, wondering what he was doing right now, wondering whether he was unhappy without me. I would spend the whole time alone, not being alone, but just thinking about him.

I saw practically no one at all the first summer we separated. My mother was in Paris so in fact I just saw her every evening and she provided that element of human communication which I think is probably necessary in the most solitary existences.

ANDREW SINCLAIR: We keep quite close. I telephone her when I am having coffee in the kitchen. If ever Marianne sounds in despair, I come round. Paris is more difficult but I could always be there in four hours. If there is a moment of despair or melancholy or real loneliness I can be with her. I can always hear it in her voice.

MARIANNE SINCLAIR: Meeting each other is certainly something to look forward to. The urge to dress and please and attract becomes so strong that one does it for one's husband alone rather than for other men at parties. I get tarted up, and dressed, and it gives me a chance to reassess my infinite attractiveness, if we have not met for some time.

ANDREW SINCLAIR: Marianne is a glowing centre and a lot of heads roll for her. We have fantastic meetings. Everything becomes new and odd, suddenly she is a stranger wandering in again. This suddenly meeting makes things much better and extraordinary. Separation makes sex much more exciting. This is the thing. It is better to worry a bit and feel a little jealous and just not be too sure. It is better than a week or two of boredom, when life is just so dead.

Marianne has always been rather a harem anyway, changing her hair colour and her way of dressing. I never quite know whom I'm going to bed with, with Marianne.

MARIANNE SINCLAIR: Andrew is very happy that I was so happy by myself. Because in a way it is a recompense for him for all the effort he had made to give me a *raison d'être* outside marriage and a home.

A child might help, but I don't think we will ever agree about this. I have always been fiendishly opposed and Andrew was rather for, at the very beginning. Now we have changed positions. I am no longer quite so dead against, but Andrew is now totally opposed.

Besides, I don't feel confident enough yet about my newly-won independence. The act of having a child would plunge me back into the state of dependence I was in when I first met Andrew. I would again be at a total disadvantage – all the independence would suddenly go because I would have to look after a child the whole time. If Andrew went away it would be marvellous for him. But I would be a wife and mother whose husband was away. I couldn't possibly feel a single and independent girl.

I stave off the question by thinking that there is plenty of time to think about it. The time of reckoning hasn't really come. The time of reckoning will come the day I am thirty-five or thirty-seven or something, not a young girl, and say to myself, it's now or never. But for the time being all one wants to do is to postpone it.

ANDREW SINCLAIR: Most women want a baby, Marianne does not, although she likes small girls. A childless marriage gives both man and wife freedom of movement, together or apart. They can choose to stay with each other or leave. Children bind people down, not together. When Brendan Behan said that he was all the children his wife needed he could be sure of her whole attention, until she had a child.

We do travel well together and that's the most difficult accomplishment in the world. We travel very hard, great distances. People intrude too much at home, but the moment you get off in a bubble, it's fine. Travel is the best bubble of all, particularly in a country where you don't know the language. You are totally enclosed.

MARIANNE SINCLAIR: It's all beautiful in the present, the past is very nice, but I don't know what it will lead to. Are we heading for ultimate togetherness or is it leading to non-marriage?

The only hypocrisy that can come about is if we refused to admit that one is inevitably and invariably jealous of someone else. I wouldn't be true to myself if I pretended that I wouldn't be jealous and miserable if Andrew started a long-lasting affair with somebody else. That has to come, and when the day comes I will have to face it and fight it with whatever weapons I have then. But it's pointless my saying that by the time he is forty-five and starts an affair with some marvellous person of twenty, I won't feel very embittered.

ANDREW SINCLAIR: Six years have passed and there is nobody else. How do you get anyone to replace six years of totally shared past? Some things should be totally known and totally unpredictable at the same time. So when the stranger comes in, he's also the lover. I'd rather be Marianne's lover, which I am now, than her husband. It's a much more interesting situation anyway, than being a husband.

MARIANNE SINCLAIR: The side of Andrew that discards me is the part of him I have always respected. I have always admired him most as a writer and as a serious dedicated person, and I want him to evolve in that direction. Also, my acceptance of the situation gave me a chance to feel gratitude to him when he said, 'Oh God, you are probably the only girl who would stand this.' I would think, perhaps I am. No mistress would stand suddenly being ditched for three months.

I think that the difference between Andrew and I is that Andrew has never put happiness at a premium. But I would choose happiness every time.

Veronica and Micky

The Situation. A Common-Law marriage between partners of different race and differing social and educational backgrounds. The couple have been living together for two years with the wife's young children by her legal husband.

The Common-Law Husband. Micky, in his mid-forties, is first generation British. He is half Japanese, his father was an immigrant who came to this country before he was born and his mother is London-born British. He left elementary school at fourteen and is employed as a mechanical engineer. He is a Communist Party member.

The Common-Law Wife. Veronica, in her mid-thirties. She comes from a northern working-class background and is the first member of her family on either side to attend university. She is an arts graduate. During her legal marriage she was an activist member of the Communist Party.

The Place. A small flat in a London neighbourhood due for slum clearance.

VERONICA: Late one evening waiting at the bus stop I saw a man standing under a street lamp doing *The Times* crossword. Getting into conversation with him I realized within half an hour that this was someone whose experience of life paralleled my own very closely. On the bus I gave him my telephone number and within two days he had moved in and was living with me. We have been together for two and a half years.

MICKY: It all went immediately right, as I knew it would. I had this peculiar feeling – a sharp physical attraction the minute we first met, then talking to her the attraction deepened. 'This I have got to have', I thought.

VERONICA: My previous marriage had broken up and I had come to London determined to succeed. I got myself a reasonably well-paid job teaching. High standards were kept up all round at home. The housework was done efficiently, the children were always washed and clean, the bills were paid on the day they arrived. I was determined that never would I say on a Saturday that I wouldn't change the beds, and go and do something else nicer. I thought that once I stopped changing the beds on Saturday we would All Go Downhill. When Micky came he said relax. I think it was the oriental Japanese in him. It was just in time because I was turning into a bit of a harpy.

At the time when I met him I was having an affair with some trappings of luxury and romance. But it paled into insignificance the moment I felt that here was somebody so warm and comforting, so everything I needed at that time. I rang this other fellow and said, 'We're finished, stop it, drop it.' I knew Micky was not just another man to add to the list, which he could have been, as I was scouring round for people who could be useful to me, people to fill in the gaps.

The moment Micky moved in I knew this was something quite different, much deeper, much more passionate and all-pervading on every level. His love-making informed his attitudes towards me throughout the whole day.

MICKY: Before I met her, on the few occasions when I felt promiscuous and had temporary arrangements with other women it was nothing like as satisfying. Sex with her means a lot to me.

She is really a very highly civilized person, but in some ways she is so narrow in her attitudes. It is partly due to her formal education being compressed into too rigid a syllabus. She wishes she had experienced a broader type of education with more emphasis on the humanities, and the arts. I have brought her one or two new interests, especially music and drawing. She didn't think she could draw but I said you don't know until you have tried. She painted a lively fish still-life.

Home comforts were never important to people like myself in the revolutionary movement, but I had a comfortable childhood and I always possessed a sense of rightness about food and the arrangement of things at home. I can go without, as I did in the early days of the Party, but I prefer to enjoy the comfortable life.

VERONICA: I married when I was twenty and still at university. I never had a well-paid job until now because my husband and I didn't think it was right. We thought we should give our all for the Revolution.

The reason I went so far out to the left was from political conviction and an attempt to halt the rot, thinking I could. My mother's family were dedicated Socialists and founder-members of the Labour Party. When I was fourteen I used to see the nationalized industry signs going up and I thought on the basis of what my mother had taught me that the millennium was here.

At home my husband and I used to pass each other on the stairs and leave each other hastily scribbled notes, 'Gone to the Trades Union Council. Dinner in oven.' Whilst we both thought this was an admirable situation at the time, we didn't realize how cold and barren our relationship had become until suddenly it was put under pressures and then we had no strength to withstand them.

We got into debt, at the same time we were having difficulties and troubles in the Party, and he became deeply depressed.

I had been going off him because having produced two babies I had suddenly lost my independence. Before, we had both led separate political lives, impinging upon each other but both fairly satisfying. Then suddenly mine was cut off. I was left at home evening after evening with the children, going quietly mad.

My husband met a girl he had known a long time ago. She relied upon him and turned to him sympathetically in a way I was incapable of at that period. After a time they went off together, and I came to London thinking that if we were going to settle our differences, distance would be an advantage.

MICKY: My parents had always assumed I would go into the family catering business – we had a restaurant – and took the view that for this job I needed only to be able to read and write. So I left elementary school at fourteen, and because of this and probably because of my origins a very limited amount of work was open to me. I flitted from one job to another until I was about fifteen when I went into engineering, non-apprenticed.

My wife was a British girl of working-class origin from my area. Her father was an unskilled worker and as a child she remembered moments of great poverty. She used to tell me about the days when the stores at home were reduced to a tin of condensed milk and a bit of margarine. She had an absolute dread of financial insecurity. I wasn't particularly successful as a breadwinner, which partly led to the break-up of our marriage. For the last ten years of our marriage she went out to work. She was unqualified and didn't even know shorthand but she has worked her way up into a position of some responsibility in a semi-technical capacity. We had four children, the marriage had lasted nineteen years when it finally broke up. It was then that I met Veronica.

VERONICA: When I was married I had one nostalgic regret. Other women used to go out shopping with their husbands on Saturday mornings wheeling the kids. But my husband was never ever there. I did the shopping on my own. I have never had a married life in which I have had so much to do with my husband. I was amazed, astounded, when Micky first said, 'I'll drive you to work, that's what a car is for', or, 'I'll be there to pick you up at five o'clock', or, 'Don't worry, I'll do it.' When I say, 'Damn, I've come to bed and left such and such in the sitting-room', he says, 'I'll get it.' I have never been so mollycoddled.

We don't have rows and this is marvellous because my husband and I couldn't have any sort of discussion without it developing into a polemical battleground. Our only problem is that Micky gets mad when I try to explain to him the ABC of subjects he knows by heart. 'Don't treat me like a class of backward children', he cries.

MICKY: I don't know to what extent my solicitous behaviour is due to my oriental background. I may have acquired these attitudes from my father. In common with many other immigrants he was living in a strange new society and he thought that this was what you had to do to be accepted. I think he imagined that the English husband was at all times courtly and courteous. A very Japanese assessment of the English.

In any case, I spend more time at home than she does. I take the children to school and Veronica to her work in the mornings, and on days when I don't go to my workshop I come home and tidy the place. Today, for example, I did out the living-room. In the afternoon I went fishing in Epping Forest for live fish-bait for a friend of mine. I did the shopping for supper, picked up Veronica from work in the car, collected the children, drove us all home, and cooked the evening meal. The kitchen is my province mainly, I enjoy cooking. We eat a lot of Japanese dishes which my parents used to enjoy, and for these I use quick cooking methods such as deep frying and boiling. French bourgeois cooking will always keep women chained to the stove because of the lengthy processes involved and I don't think the results are worth it.

VERONICA: The difference between his dish of eggs and bacon and mine is the art of gastronomy. Luckily, I have to fight to get near the cooker. But in general it is not a question of his darting about the house all day in a frilly apron while I'm out earning the money. The person who happens to have the time available that day does the housework and the shopping. When he is working, I do it.

When Micky turned up I had already had a flat for eighteen months, with the lease in my name. I was enjoying financial security and signing my own cheques in a way I had never experienced previously. In no way did I throw myself on him and say, 'Support me and my children', and this independence has been maintained. I still pay the rent, the electricity, the monthly bills and all the things I used to pay for. Micky's money provides the extras, the car, the petrol, the tax, and whatever luxuries we need such as good cuts of meat from the butcher and holidays together.

My children are now pretty well my sole responsibility. Their father did send me in the early days an allowance of four to five pounds a week but the sum is reduced now and arrives only intermittently. I don't go to him for shoes and clothes because now he has a young family of his own to look after himself. I clothe my children and Micky feeds them.

MICKY: Money is a problem as far as my relationship with my first wife is concerned. She doesn't get any from me. My two boys are working, my older girl will shortly be earning her own living, and the youngest one who often comes to see us is fourteen. But all the children are self-sufficient and capable of looking after themselves. My ex-wife is now living with a much younger man but she is in no hurry to give up her independence – although he would like her to.

VERONICA: I have never felt bitter towards my husband. In a way my children have two fathers. They spend at least a month in the summer with their father and his new family. The kids talk to him about Micky and say, 'He can make a penny disappear', and their father comes back with, 'Ah, but can he make a handkerchief go right through one ear and come out the other?' The children talk a lot about their half brothers and sisters whom they like.

The children had known the mother of their half brothers and sisters as a friend, and her present relationship with their father dawned on them gradually. There was no traumatic shock.

MICKY: I am now a self-employed mechanical engineer, but I'm not formally qualified. I decided I wanted to be out of the factory. With my ability to design tools I decided the best way to improve myself was to set up on my own. I have earned considerably more than Veronica over the last two years but I have been paying back old debts. When my marriage broke up I got depressed, I didn't go to work and the bills piled up as usual. The fact that I know I can earn reasonably large sums of money tends to make me lazy. I would earn a lot more if I worked harder.

VERONICA: My father was an electrical engineer, also unqualified like Micky. Indulgent parents didn't make him stick at his apprenticeship so he never became qualified. Therefore all his life he suffered from the fact that he could do more than the men who were in charge at the factory where he worked. Many women meet and love a man who is like their own father.

My working-class background has given me roots and an understanding of life which is denied to people who have always been a little bit suburban and middle-class, or who have been sheltered from the money point of view. I can't shed this, nor do I want to. I do realize that my conscious rejection of some working-class values makes me middle-class in a somewhat jejune sense. In choosing, for example, to drink wine with Sunday dinner, and taking the *Observer*, I differ from my mother. But I do consider myself to be working-class, and so does my younger brother. He was one of the lads among the chaps at Oxford and is now a university lecturer. I think it takes two or three generations for people to move out of a working-class background through education.

My political life has been one of progressive disillusion. It was only after years of giving up money and leisure and friends for the movement which produced sweet nothing did I begin to think it was better to move out and wait until the time is right for us all to go and do something. *Cultivez votre jardin.* But not to work, work, work when the political situation didn't warrant it.

Our political convictions are unchanged and we support the Party. I think we would both be more actively involved in local government if the local situation were not so hopeless, politically. But we both continue to attend party rallies and many of the meetings.

In London, the Party is more middle-class and intellectual. Many more of the meetings are cultural meetings, down here. The first folk song revival was organized by the Party in London.

Up in Liverpool, we tended to call all that typical bourgeois, a frittering away of valuable time. We had the real problems on our hands, we thought. We were interested in the workers. We were all workers, of course, but one or two of us had been to university and felt we might not have had proper working-class experience. But we apologized for it.

I would like lots of money but I don't intend to slave for it. I don't intend to narrow down my life and lose what I have gained over the last two years, my capacity for enjoyment, by chasing money.

If I had money I would like lots of lovely modern furniture in advanced designs, I would like to be able to buy many books, the large glossy art books I see in bookshops but don't even think of buying. Most of all I would like to be able to look at the menu in an expensive restaurant without thinking, fifteen bob for an omelet when eggs are only fourpence each!

MICKY: We share our political convictions. My own attachment to the Communist movement began when I was a boy of about fourteen. Also, the pressures of the day were working. It was in 1936–39 and during the Spanish Civil War and Munich period.

I feel I owe the Party a lot. Over my whole period as a

member I have met such a wide variety of people whom I could never have met in other circumstances. Also, the Party has broadened and stimulated my cultural interests. My overall position is one of unchanging loyalty, but I am not going to devote my life to the Party until the political situation justifies it.

Apart from politics, we share a deep love of the countryside, we try to spend as much time as we can camping. We like driving round town late in the evening when the streets are deserted so we can look at the architecture, we like to creep about old parts of London down by the docks.

We like to feel free to do what we like when we like. Sometimes I do think a bit romantically about what our own child would be like. I'm curious to know. But I've had enough children, four of my own, and now these two of hers – I have a good relationship with them, with the boy specially.

During my first marriage, neither of our mothers were willing baby-sitters, so the whole time we took the children everywhere with us. It was absolute hell, especially when they were young. Quite apart from the expense involved, there was the nervous wear and tear of constantly shepherding this brood.

VERONICA: I don't want to go back to four-hourly feeds and nappies. Soon after Micky first moved in I found I was pregnant, to my surprise. I didn't think I was easy to impregnate. At first I was full of hazy romantic notions about how delightful, how lovely. Even when I began to feel very sick, I thought I can cope, I have coped with so much during these past two years.

Then I realized, no I cannot cope, and when I spontaneously aborted at three months I was relieved. I remained at home until I knew there was no chance of saving the foetus, and then I rang the hospital and went in for a D and C. That finished it. I don't want any more now.

MICKY: I don't know why we don't get married. I'm free to.

Sometime ago my wife said, 'I'm going to divorce you', and I replied, 'I don't blame you', and she did. We were on pretty good terms and we still are. She hasn't remarried and this divorce has been the making of her.

VERONICA: It has been the making of many a woman to be rid of her husband.

I rang my husband to ask him whether he would like to get divorced and remarry so as to legitimize his four children, but he declined. He said, 'Not really, Daphne is a bit difficult and I think that marriage would disturb our relationship.' So I haven't bothered to pursue the idea further. I really don't see why I should. He met Micky one evening and the whole thing went like a bomb.

My present marriage has enabled me to keep the financial independence I value so much and the feeling of pulling my weight. At the same time, Micky has made my life richer and warmer by sharing many of the physical difficulties which could well have been a burden without him, such as playing his part in the discipline and care of the children and in every way being a partner. I like it this way.

2. *The priority of children*

Mark and Jessica

The Situation. A young couple who want to produce a child have had no luck. Six years of marriage pass before they decide on adoption.

The Husband. Mark, aged twenty-nine, managing director of the family building firm in a provincial city. He was educated at grammar school and went straight into the family business.

The Wife. Jessica, aged thirty. She is the daughter of a local alderman, educated at a private day school. She is a trained shorthand-typist.

The Place. A modern detached house in a leafy suburb of Huddersfield.

JESSICA: We had been married six years and all our friends were having babies – three or four babies – and for us there was nothing. I hated hearing about all these people who were continually getting pregnant. One particular girl friend produced a child almost every year and I used to be in tears when she told me she was expecting another. I was watching every month. If ever my period was a day or two late or if I felt a bit sick in the mornings, I used to get quite excited.

Life seemed very sterile without children. I'm not a religious person but I used to think, if there is a God he has been jolly rotten to me, what have I done to deserve this?

I was working when we first married but I gave it up after a year when we went to live in Huddersfield. All the time I kept thinking, I'll probably be pregnant and there is not much point getting another job. Besides, people used to say to me, 'If you stay at home and relax you are much more likely to conceive.' Looking back I can't think what I did to fill the day, but I did, and I was never really bored. We have a big house and a garden, and we had planned the nursery.

MARK: I was twenty-two when I got married and Jessica was twenty-three. She was a secretary, but after about a year I insisted she gave up her job, largely because I got fed up with getting out of bed to drive her to the station.

We never made any attempt not to have children. Jessica didn't use any contraceptives, and neither did I. After a while we began to think it was a bit odd that everybody else had children and we had not. There was obviously something wrong.

I went to a doctor because I thought possibly there was something wrong with me, and I had the usual embarrassing tests. The doctor said, 'No, there is nothing wrong with you, you should be able to have children.'

For a long time there was a hiatus in which I was worried about telling Jessica that it was her. An extra sense of urgency inevitably entered into our love-making, but it wasn't a case of doggedly dragging her off to bed early because by God, this time we are going to make it. Sex for us has never been that unspontaneous. We made love about three or four times a week, but we didn't make love more than we would have done normally.

Eventually, I told her, 'As a matter of fact there is nothing wrong with me, so I am afraid it must be you.' Until my tests I had been very worried, partly because I had contracted mumps during my formative years and people do say 'Oh, you'll never do it now.' At this stage Jessica went along to see a train of doctors and specialists. The doctors did all these embarrassing tests on her too and said, 'There is no reason why you can't have children, none at all.' Then one of the specialists said that there may be a psychological reason why she is not conceiving, she is not in the right frame of mind for conception.

JESSICA: They did say to me that though I look quite calm

on the outside I'm chewed up and nervy and tense inside, and I was told that this was not conducive to my chances of conceiving.

I went to a psychoanalyst for about a year and a half. My analyst thought there might be some block – there is a view that the ability to conceive is influenced by subconscious mental attitudes. I hated being analysed at first, but I got used to it after a while. You can get used to anything in the end. I kept thinking, it's worth it if the method works and I get a baby. Sometimes I was given injections, to relax me and to make me talk the truth. The drugs sent me to sleep and half of what he asked me and what I said I don't know. He asked me in my conscious moments about my childhood and 'Did you have any experiences with nasty men when you were little?' and all that.

When I came away I always used to feel very relaxed. I staggered home and went to bed. I couldn't walk properly. It was like being drunk.

It didn't help at all, it was a waste of time, or so I thought, as it didn't seem to do the trick.

MARK: She became rather neurotic. She became introverted and worried about herself. The analyst cost five guineas an hour, plus the cost of the drugs, and what was distressing was that Jessica got terribly upset about being analysed. It was an intrusion on her. We just went on more and more worriedly as time passed and the analyst didn't turn up anything. The analyst kept calling me in and giving me little talks on sexual technique, all of which I knew already. Almost everything he suggested I had already tried. He recommended a couple of books which although they considerably increased the pleasure of love-making didn't do the trick.

JESSICA: It has been mentioned to us that the fact that both of us are overweight is a factor, but the tests proved conclusively that it is not his fault. Right from the beginning, I accepted that it was my fault.

MARK: The curious thing is that up to about two years ago neither of us ever mentioned adopting a child. I was loath to bring up the idea because it implied that we had given up the prospect of having a child of our own. But it occurred to me that we couldn't afford, on any level, to continue with Jessica's weekly analysis.

So I said, 'Love, how do you feel about adopting a child?' And it turned out she had been trying to think of a way to put it to me too. You never really know the person to whom you are married, you never really do, ever. I never guessed she had been sitting there, biting her nails and thinking, how am I going to phrase it?

We kept our decision quiet, saying nothing to anybody, because the process of adoption is long-drawn-out and hazardous.

We went to all the normal agencies, the National Children's Adoption Society, the National Society for the Adoption of this that and the other, and they said all the usual things they say and you get the impression that it all boils down to, 'Do you go to church or not?' Neither of us does. This is one of the cruel anomalies of the adoption procedure – you must be a churchgoer. So acute is the situation that I believe that there is a new agency formed for non-believers with a long list of prospective adopters. Like me, people don't see why the hell they should go to church or lie about it in order to be able to adopt. Even if you do lie, it's no good because the society gets in touch with your local vicar to check. Even then, assuming you go to church, with the recognized adoption societies there was a two-year delay when we wanted to adopt.

We were nearly twenty-seven and twenty-eight years old and we didn't relish the prospect of waiting until our middle thirties before we had a child. So I went to a private agency I knew of – third-party adoptions, which are very unpopular with the authorities.

The agency went through just as many long-winded checks as the established societies, first of all wanting to know why we couldn't have one, then we had to go to the doctor and establish that we were healthy and unlikely to drop dead the day after adopting. After about three or four months, they told us, 'You have been accepted as prospective adopters.'

'What kind of a child would be your ideal, what would you really like better than anything else?' we were asked. I replied that I honestly didn't mind, I just wanted a family. I said I wouldn't mind having a coloured child, but Jessica, after a lot of heart-searching, said she didn't think she could love a coloured child as much as she could a white one. The agency told us that it was hard enough adopting in the ordinary run of events without imposing the extra handicap of having a coloured child unless the adopters specially wanted one. So we said, 'Okay, in that case we want an Anglo-Saxon child which looks as much like us as possible.' At that time, we said we wanted a girl, I didn't mind, but Jessica preferred a girl.

During the following six months a number of people both from the agency and local authorities came to visit us to ascertain that neither of us were drunk at eleven o'clock in the morning. Suddenly, there would be a knock on the door and there was the local Child Care Officer wanting to look round the house and check that the bathroom was clean and there were no smalls hanging in the lav.

Finally, we got a phone call and the agency man said, 'Would you like a boy?' and I almost dropped the phone. I said, 'What, what, what, Jessica, would you like a boy?'

JESSICA: I dreaded going to see him. I don't automatically like every baby I lay eyes on, and I thought how dreadful to have to say to the foster-mother, 'I don't like that child.' The relief when I did like him! I remember seeing this tiny little thing with huge blue eyes and thinking he is really very sweet.

Our first meeting was decidedly unpleasant. The foster-mother sat there all the time and held him herself and she made us feel uncomfortable. I got this horrible impression that it was like going into a supermarket and buying a packet of cornflakes. He was two weeks old. We looked at him and liked him and that was it.

MARK: To me, it wasn't any different from having a child of my own. This is a very important thing. Like every other father, I saw him when he was very tiny and then he came home a few weeks later. It was just as if he had been kept a little longer in hospital. I don't know what effect this had on Jessica because I don't know how deeply she wanted the physical experience of motherhood – there are emotional involvements in the case of a woman, which men don't feel, in the actual physical process of giving birth.

What followed was quite the worst period of my life, where we waited for three months for the child to become legally ours. He was at home, but he was not actually ours.

JESSICA: While we were waiting for him to arrive I kept thinking, 'Have we done the right thing?' When you are pregnant you get nine months of swelling and thinking about how you are going to cope with a new baby. But for me, one day I hadn't got a baby, and the next day – still in exactly the same shape and state – I had a baby. As soon as we got him home, Mark took a week off work to get to know his son, that was very important.

I was terrified when we first had him home. I felt so in-effectual, especially when he cried. Half the time I didn't know what I was doing.

MARK: She was overtense about him because she felt she ought to love him but somehow there wasn't something soft and pink happening inside her, there were no violins playing outside the nursery window. At first she said she couldn't feel about him as if he were a child of our own. But the moment he was actually ours her attitude changed completely.

Up to that time she was worried. One night when I came home she said, 'I don't think I can love him, he will have to go back.' I was dreadfully upset because I became committed to him almost from the first moment I saw him. I think I would have gone off my nut if the mother had wanted him returned.

We went through the ordeal of waiting outside the court and going to see the judge. He asked us a number of questions. Then it all happened in thirty seconds. The judge pronounced that he had looked into our case. 'I have decided,' he said, 'the child is now yours.' From that moment he was really ours, the Law said so, and his mother from that moment onwards had no legal claim on him whatsoever. It was simply a biological accident that she happened to have him in the first place.

JESSICA: That first month of having him at home absolutely exhausted me. Mark was very good and understanding about it, I would go to bed on alternate nights at about eight o'clock and go to sleep and Mark would give the baby his ten o'clock feed while he watched television. By the time he wanted his two o'clock bottle I had managed to put in some sleep. But by the time I'd got back to bed at dawn the beastly birds would start and I'd lie awake for about two hours, and I'd just be dropping off when he would wake up for the next feed. And I'm a person who needs a good night's sleep. It used to take me a whole day to give him his bottles and keep up with the washing and ironing in spite of the fact that we do have a washing-machine.

MARK: One of the curious aspects of adopting is that the mother doesn't get any of the prenatal training available to a natural mother. The adopting mother has to go out and find out for herself. We had a stack of books so high on the subject, but even so, the first night we had the baby with us was paralysing. I woke up in the early morning – no sign of Jessica. Silence. I hadn't been wakened at all during the night or heard a sound out of the baby. I thought, he's dead, we've strangled him, or done something wrong and he has died. I shot out of bed like a cork out of a bottle and rushed upstairs to the nursery expecting to find a lifeless baby and that Jessica had shot herself dead by the cot or something. But the baby was perfectly all right, lying there happily gurgling away. In fact, he had woken up once in the night and she had gone up to him and then when he was settled again she went back into the spare room so as not to disturb me.

JESSICA: When it was his birthday in June it was the first time for a long time I didn't think of him as being mine because I remembered, what is his mother thinking today? To me his birthday was last Saturday, though we didn't celebrate it in any way, we had had him the full year.

As soon as he was legally ours I never thought of sending him back, not even when he bawled and bawled, not that he did that very often because he has been a very good child. If he had been excessively naughty I suppose I might have harboured those thoughts every now and again.

He gets car-sick and I said to Mark, 'Why should he be car-sick when neither of us are sick in cars?' And then I realized that he might get the weakness from his biological mother or father. I had almost forgotten that he doesn't inherit our tendencies.

We know about his mother, we have to, but she doesn't know about us. She knows what our income is and what kind of people we are. The fear is always vaguely at the back of my mind that one day she will turn up. When I see a glamorous brunette I often wonder if she might be his mother, because I gather that's what she is like. I know she lives in Manchester and works in an office.

MARK: I wanted a son and now I've got him and he couldn't be a more perfect son for me if Jessica had produced him. He is one of the happiest children I've ever seen. He's fantastically good-looking – this isn't just me – people stop me in the street and say what a beautiful baby and it boosts your ego.

Having him has relaxed me. What used to irritate me was the thought that I was worried about what other people were thinking – 'Poor things, they can't have a baby.' Normally, I don't give a damn what other people think. But I began to worry about the fact that I hadn't proved myself a man because I hadn't got a child. Men have this feeling that they ought to be able to produce children, even if their wife is barren. I felt that I ought to be potent enough to give her a child despite everything.

JESSICA: When you have a child you feel that life is more worth living. You don't feel so selfish. Mark is earning money to give our baby a good start in life rather than just spending the money on ourselves on nothing in particular.

We are waiting to adopt another, a girl this time, and I'm getting panicky about it in my usual way. Also, I have had another internal examination and a D and C and they told me at the hospital that there is still no reason why I should not conceive. We have been married seven years and you hear of people going as much as twelve years and suddenly producing a baby. We still could.

Janice Waller

The Situation. A young working-class wife grapples with married life and motherhood within the context of cramped accommodation in a house occupied by her in-laws.

The Wife. Janice Waller, aged twenty-eight. She is married to George Waller, a painter-decorator, aged thirty-three. They have been married for nine years and have twin boys of four years.

The Place. A basement flat in Wandsworth.

JANICE: Georgie was my first boy and my only one. I'd known him almost from the time I left school. I got engaged when I was nearly seventeen, and we got married three years after that. I married because I loved him.

We shared a house with my husband's parents. We had two rooms, a bedroom upstairs and the front room, and in the basement a weeny kitchen next door to a condemned room. One corner was quite damp, and Georgie put some stuff up and that kept it back a lot but when it rained that complete wall used to be damp. Down there it was always dark and you always had to have the light on. It was a very small kitchen with one tiny window, about eighteen inches. Georgie knocked it all down and made a big window and moved the sink so I looked out of the window. But first off I had my sink against the flat wall and that was depressing.

We went there because Georgie and I was going to save. When we first went they only charged us £1 which wasn't too bad, but then it crept up to £3.

I worked until I was seven months with the twins. It was a question of getting the money together, so I couldn't give up. I was supposed to give up at four months because at the hospital they said the swellings were getting too much.

I had the twins at ten o'clock in the morning and I wouldn't let them ring my sister because my sister is one of those who talks a lot, and then everyone would have known before Georgie. So when Georgie came at half past seven he didn't know until then I'd had them. He was thrilled because I'd waited to tell him first. He wanted a boy from the start, and then we had the two. That was the only night he didn't bring me anything, not a bit of fruit, not a flower, nothing. He was very upset about that.

I never had any hot water at his Mum's, so we had to boil kettles up. To give the twins a bath I'd have to boil one kettle for one lot of bath water, and then I'd have to wait for the kettle for the second one. Then there were the bottles to do. I never finished putting the kettle on.

Being the first babies, I wouldn't have a bottle ready, I'd always make it fresh. If I had another one it wouldn't get as much treatment as they got. I don't believe in all this cotton-wool business, and separate things for this and that. But being the first, you sort of accept it.

I didn't believe in those disposable nappies so I had fourteen nappies a day. I took the white wash to the local baths where I could do the lot for 2/6d. I couldn't afford the launderette, as

I had so much. But the woollens I did myself every day. I used to have to wash their night-dresses at night to keep the washing down. There was nowhere to hang them to dry so I used to put them on the fire-guard away from the fire every night.

The twins were always getting dirty or being sick and I couldn't bear babies with sick on them. As soon as they were sick, the cardigan had to come off.

It used to get me down, especially being up most of the night with them. When we first had them home, Georgie used to feed one of the evening. But after the excitement wore off, he'd never get up of a night-time because he had to go to work the next day. If he couldn't sleep the whole night, he'd get a bit annoyed.

With the two, we found it really hard at first – especially as we weren't expecting twins. We got the extra grant, but it didn't go anywhere. Georgie used to give me £12 housekeeping. That covered £3 rent, and the rest for coal, electricity, gas and the television, and insurance. He kept about £4 for himself. But as he didn't smoke or drink most of it went on petrol and the car – he worked ever so hard and had ever so many jobs. He never liked the basement and rather than stay in and be with me, he would go out and do the work that came up to earn the money.

My in-laws disliked the twins using the garden. They never picked the flowers but they used to make a mess. They loved to pick up the dirt, and they had their toys out there and he didn't like it because it looked a mess. I couldn't let them out in the yard. It was horrible summer-time with the dustbins, the smell and the flies.

So I had to restrict them to indoors. They used to play in the passage a lot, but then my in-laws used to get annoyed and start shouting, 'Why can't you keep the children quiet?' If they could have made mud pies in the garden they would have been quiet and you wouldn't hear a sound out of them. I used to sit down and try and read them a story, but they wanted to be out.

I only had to leave them for a minute and being the two of them, they started to fight and cry and once they start they do scream. As soon as I went into the toilet they started crying or banging on the door which I got really upset about at first. As soon as I'd got in there I'd have to rush out again before I'd more or less sat down.

In the summer it was, I left my dinner ready and I asked my mother-in-law to put the dinner on. We had a flighty gas stove and it set fire to the plastic curtain above and the whole kitchen was burned out, all our furniture and everything. From then on we had to go upstairs and share her kitchen. It was all right for the first couple of weeks but after a while my in-laws kept coming and switching the tap off every time I started doing a bit of washing – they started counting how many times I used the sink.

When they were two and a half the twins had a mania for breaking the milk bottles in the passage with the milk in. They would pick up the bottles and go, clink! They liked the sound of it and the two bottles used to smash. This went on for about a week and Georgie said, 'For goodness sake take the milk in as soon as it comes.' But I was so busy I never took it in. One day my mother-in-law came in just as they had done it. I'd got to the seventh day and I had smacked them for doing it. My mother-in-law, she was really upset, she says 'You shouldn't have smacked him like that.' And I very calmly said, 'Mum, you go upstairs and leave me to bring my children up.' My father-in-law was in that day and he called out 'Come up Vi, they are Janice's children and you leave it to her.' It could have turned nasty if I had lost my temper. To this day I don't know how I kept so calm because I was seething inside.

Georgie is very close to his family but I wouldn't say he put them first. He would take my part first. He used to say to his

Dad, 'Why don't you come and tell me instead of always picking on Janice? She's got a hard enough job down there with the two kids all day, looking after them and keeping them quiet.' But if I was in the wrong, he'd tell me.

The twins slept in our bedroom – because our other room was downstairs. I wouldn't have minded having them in a next-door room, but not right downstairs. I was never very keen on love because I always felt it might wake them up. They are very light sleepers and you only have to cough for them to wake. As they got older the situation got worse. I'm not saying we didn't do it because we did. It didn't seem to affect George very much – he doesn't worry about it as I do. He doesn't get upset if the children are awake whereas it spoils it for me if they should wake up in the middle. George says they are too young to know anyway, but I couldn't see it like that.

Then Georgie had a bad attack of nerves. His father asked us if we could find other accommodation and said he would like us out by December, and Georgie was worried about where we were going to go. We tried so hard and we couldn't get a place. In the end Georgie didn't think we were going to get anywhere. We didn't stand a chance wherever we went – once they knew we had the twins, they just didn't want to know us.

Georgie talked about killing himself, but he didn't really want to leave us behind. We used to have long talks and I used to sit up most of the night with him, I would never go to sleep before he did in case he did go out and do anything. I couldn't go for an hour without being shouted at.

The doctor said, he had to get out of it himself. Georgie couldn't shift himself off the chair. He didn't work for about two months and we hadn't got anything saved then with the twins and everything. My mother was pretty good, she used to give me quite a bit of food and my sister who lives across the road used to help. My father-in-law let us leave the rent.

Then we were lucky. The woman who lived a couple of doors away from us heard of a flat. She knew we were getting a bit near the deadline.

We pay £24 a month rent which is due on the twelfth day so we've worked it out at about £5 10s. a week. We've got four rooms, a kitchen, a bathroom and toilet. We've not got much of a garden but there is a beautiful yard for the twins which they can't get out of.

A friend, she wasn't a friend at the time but she is now, said her little girl had started going to the play-group in the park and she was three, and she liked it. Well, the twins were coming up three and when I went the lady said they had a few vacancies. I was lucky there. The play-group used to keep them from nine thirty until twelve every morning and I had no trouble leaving them because they had each other.

Now I have got a permanent part-time job of working for the play-group and I'm doing a college course with it. I get 27s. per session and I do five mornings, so it helps. But Georgie wouldn't like it if it upset the children, and if it did, I wouldn't do the job.

The twins played me up when I first started working at the play-group as a relief assistant, because they thought they could get away with everything, but they can't. Now they realize it's not much different from home, they're doing better.

On a Tuesday when I go to the lectures, Georgie will put them to bed for me. And he will make sure they eat their tea up because I have to leave at half past six. If I was to go out a lot he'd be upset. He doesn't say much when I am in, but if I'm not around he is a bit, 'Well, where have you been?'

I only get paid once a month so, as I have just started, I haven't really benefited yet. When I get paid I will give Georgie some money to save. I ought to help Georgie out because for five years he's kept us and we've never really wanted for much. I could never say to him I wish I could have had so and so, because what I've more or less wanted Georgie

has tried to give us. We spoil the boys a bit too much sometimes, especially about cars and things. Every week he buys
them a present. Every Sunday he gets them a comic and he
never buys the twins anything without buying me something.
It might just be a box of chocolates or some nice pears, only
something small. I never get flowers. Georgie doesn't like
carrying flowers. What I've always wanted is to get a big
bouquet through the door. I had a big bouquet in hospital
when I had the boys but my mother-in-law got them for him
and carried it up for him.

George wants another baby but I wouldn't want any more
now. I had a miscarriage and I would have liked to have kept
that one. But now the twins are going to school soon, and
I'm having a different change in my life getting out and about
again and not tied in so much, I don't want any more. I was
really tied. When they were little and it was a wet day and we
couldn't go to the park I used to try and go up to my own
Mum's for a while. But I couldn't go because I couldn't get
both of them in the push-chair on a bus. The first winter, that
bad winter, we couldn't step outside the door because they
tended to be bronchial.

I will enjoy life more with me working and getting things
together.

I'd like to learn to drive but we can't afford to run two cars
and I can't see Georgie saying 'I'll walk to work today dear,
you can have the car.'

He doesn't help much about the house. He would if it came
to the pinch and I asked, but if I don't ask I don't get nothing
done. But then again I don't expect him to.

I'd never let Georgie go away to work. Sometimes, builders
get jobs living away. I didn't like being on my own for the
first three years, and since we've had the twins he's never
wanted to go so we've always been together. The only nights
we've had apart was when I was in hospital.

The only time we go out together is our anniversary, but the last couple of times we haven't made it. Last year we couldn't get anyone to look after the twins and this time we went to Georgie's cousins' wedding instead. Because my mother- and father-in-law went out every Saturday night – they like to go out for their little drink – and we couldn't expect them to sit in for us.

George likes his couple of days fishing and the twins are getting to the age when they enjoy a bit of fishing. George is not one for going to the seaside or anything, he can't bear to be in traffic jams with his car. So if we go anywhere with the twins we go somewhere quiet. Sometimes we take a ride up to the Common on a Sunday because there is a boat lake. But if the twins are not in bed before nine you can't speak to them the next day.

This year we're not having an actual holiday because I want the twins to have a really nice bedroom and Georgie is building them fitted cupboards.

Georgie is much more his old self again now. It was April Fools' Day and Georgie is terrified of spiders. I was listening to the news and the man said, 'You've got an hour if you want to do an April Fool.' We had this new toilet put in and they had taken the pipes out of the wall and when Georgie came out of the bathroom I said 'Georgie there's a great big spider on your back.' He started off by being annoyed, but he had to laugh in the end. It was the first time, he said, he'd been caught out. But a few months ago I would really have got told off for it.

I still have fourteen vests and fourteen pants to wash a week, and that's not counting Georgie's washing. To see my washing now anyone would think I'd got about ten kids. As old as they are now, they still have clean vest and pants and socks on every day. I've never been lucky enough to be given clothes for the twins that would do. People give me one, but the boys like to be dressed alike. If Tony goes out in the garden and gets dirty and I change his jumper, Michael immediately comes in and wants his jumper changed. You can't say no, because he'd think, 'What's Tony got I haven't?'

Sometimes I get depressed and I think I ought to go out and have a break. Georgie doesn't mind staying in. I'm a great talker but Georgie is not very good. He'll listen and nod, but he hasn't really got a lot he wants to say.

He never calls me the old woman or anything like that. He always says, 'This is my wife', same as I would never dream of calling him the old man. A lot of people know we are married because I am always saying Georgie this, Georgie that.

Louise and John

The Situation. A second marriage for both husband and wife. After four years of the marriage, the wife persuades her ex-husband, who has custody of their twin girl and boy, to permit the children to return to her care. Shortly after the event, the wife's health and morale cracks up. They have a daughter of nearly three.

The Second Husband. John, in his early forties. He is an accountant with a big industrial company.

The Second Wife. Louise, aged forty-one, a lapsed Roman Catholic. She comes from a middle-class family and was educated at a well-known girls' public school. During her first marriage she held a responsible professional post.

The Place. A Victorian vicarage in a commuters' village in Hertfordshire.

JOHN: Louise's breakdown was basically about guilt. Guilt about believing she was the cause of the final break-up of her first marriage, and she may have felt this especially deeply because of her Roman Catholic upbringing. The magnitude of the decision of having to choose between me and the twins, because that is what her dilemma was in fact, created a deep fissure of loyalties. She felt guilty about it all and even the birth of our daughter failed to help her to come to terms with herself.

When the children came to live with us they were very lively, not scholarly and at their most exhausting age – the girl was a real tomboy. I notice that they are much easier to control now they are a bit older.

I genuinely like the twins and I think they accept me. I had known them well from the beginning of my relationship with their mother, but I remember one particular incident on the morning after they came to live with us. The twins rushed into our bedroom early in the morning. I had great qualms. This is the scene, I thought, in which impressionable young things may begin to resent the wicked fellow who has ousted their father from the mother's bed. But although you never know how these things affect the individual psyche, all that appeared to happen was that the boy shouted to the girl, 'Race you to John's side of the bed.' They got in one on either side of me.

I was perhaps rather over-reticent about disciplining them. I was very conscious that I must not overdo it, and I tended to be mild until things got so bad I lost my temper.

LOUISE: At that time our day went like this. At half past seven a.m. the alarm goes off. Everybody rushes into our bedroom saying 'Hello', 'Good Morning', 'Where's my school tie?' This is a school morning so no time for a cuddle in bed with Didi. 'Your clothes have been put out.' 'Get into them.' 'Stop that din.' 'No, you cannot take water-pistols to school.' 'I said no.' 'Didi dress yourself.' 'I don't want to dress myself.' 'Dress yourself, come on show me how clever you are.' 'All right, I'll help you get dressed.'

I get dressed because I do the school drive. We are all downstairs for breakfast at a quarter to eight. Afterwards, 'Go to the lavatory – one up, one down!' An argument about that. 'Do your teeth.' Delaying tactics about this.

By twenty to nine we are all in the car. I drive three miles to the big children's schools, dropping off Didi at her nursery school on the way back.

On the return trip I do the shopping for the day and, if I

can't think of anything more imaginative for lunch I work on the rota of mince on Mondays, liver and bacon on Tuesdays, stew on Thursday, fish Friday, a roast on the weekend days.

When I get home I share the housework with our au pair. She is responsible for cleaning our sitting-room, the kitchen, our bedroom and bathroom. I do the stairs, the twins' room, the hall, help her polish the sitting-room floor and generally supervise as our au pair is untrained in the domestic arts. Also I do jobs like washing all the grubby finger marks off the indoor paintwork.

I do lunch which, as it is Didi's main meal of the day, is a proper two-course meal with a nursery-type pudding. The au pair washes up the things that do not go into the dishwasher, and then goes off duty for her lessons.

Half an hour's rest for mother and child. Didi sits on her potty and watches television. After this point the day's arrangements vary. Sometimes I take Didi to her dancing lesson or we go out for a walk. On a spare afternoon I might ask a girl friend with a child who is a friend of Didi's to come over to tea.

At four o'clock the twins are back with whoops, shrieks, fights. A glass of milk and a slice of cake for them before they settle down to prep for half an hour asking me questions – 'How do you spell calliper?'

At four thirty tea for the girl friend, Didi and friend and myself. We have sandwiches, biscuits and cake and milk, set out nicely as a good tea is the best part of the fun for a visiting child, and a pot of tea for the grown-ups.

Then the twins pipe up, 'Can we look at television?' There is usually a skirmish about this as, although telly provides a jolly good breather for Mum, I do not want my children going about as cowboys. I assent and, depending on the type of programme on, set a viewing-time limit. On fine days they rush into the garden and kick a ball around having first tried to coax me into coming out to play with them. I feel the need of an energetic games coach at this hour. At their boarding schools they both did games every day and loved it, but at their new day schools games are limited to twice a week.

At six o'clock, goodbye to the friend and child. Now I face the old problem. Should I organize a meal around seven o'clock which we all eat together, or should I serve supper now to the children and a later dinner for John? Family supper-times are noisy. I know that when he comes home and sees the kitchen table laid for five he will say, 'Oh, are we all eating together?' and his face will drop a mile. He needs peace. I decide on two supper-times.

After the meal, bath-time. First Didi then the twins. I do Didi and pop her into bed with a book. I still have to supervise the twins because if they are left on their own they will skip bits. It's impractical for them to bath together because we get a flood in the bathroom.

Up three flights of stairs to see if one is done and down again to keep an eye on the one not in the bathroom – then I do that one and it is up and down, up and down until they are all in bed by seven-thirty and the twins read for half an hour. I go down and have a drink with John who has been in for twenty minutes or so. Then we both go up for a final good-night story to the three children and final hugs, tolerate some nonsense from Didi who usually insists on her right to have just one more story. Then I start to cook a proper dinner, and there are still the shoes to do and some mending.

After a few weeks of this I began to feel just a dazed thing.

JOHN: I was sufficiently worried about the situation to take it into my own hands to write to the twins' father and inform him that Louise looked as if she might crack up.

Her perfectionism was partly the cause. Everything had to be perfect, a legacy she inherited from her mother. I would rather have a bit of dust lying around the house if it meant she was going to be more relaxed. She always told me that she had lowered her standards already and that she was brought up to see that the furniture was polished every day and the silver cleaned every time it was used.

But it is true that I did hate eating all together in the evenings. 7 p.m. is the low ebb of the day for me. I look forward all day to a before-dinner drink to pep me up and a quiet meal with Louise to enable me to relax. I don't do much domestic work – one of her main complaints. Honestly, I feel too tired except for gardening at the weekend. I have to get up at 7.30 a.m. in order to be in the office at 8.30 a.m. and when I come home at seven o'clock I'm dead from work trying to make money and getting pushed up in the firm.

LOUISE: I remember saying to my mother, 'I do feel so depressed', and then next day it became worse. I went to our GP, who took my blood pressure and although he found it a bit high said that nothing else serious was wrong. He prescribed some sleeping pills and a tonic.

I hoped the children wouldn't notice how I felt and of course they didn't. I just dragged myself from one job to the next without any sense of purpose. If I saw a friend in the park I went the other way behind the trees.

We went away to my sister's for the weekend, all of us. The twins woke me up at 5 a.m. and I tried to keep them quiet. I kept repeating, 'This is my bedroom, please go out again.' I felt as if I had reached the ashbase of all existence. My sister came in and said, 'Whatever can be the matter? You look marvellous. You're all right.' I lay down on the bed thinking, my God, what can I do? How can I get myself out of it? Then I put on a smile and went downstairs.

I went to an analyst, but he had, for me, such a deeply unsympathetic personality, and treated me like a fool into the bargain that after my second interview with him I knew there was no hope left. I was then quite desperate and rudderless and what I did was unforgivably irresponsible, I know that, but there seemed no way out and that is terrible. I was lucky that I was found in time. When I came round I was told that

I was being admitted to hospital for electric-shock treatment. It was no shock to me, there was no such sensation left in me at that stage.

JOHN: I contacted the twins' father and told him what had happened and asked if he could make arrangements to have the children back, at least for a while. He agreed and we were lucky enough to persuade their former school heads to take them back.

LOUISE: Now I have the twins at home for two months in the year. It is frustrating but bearable. They spend half their holidays with me. Then I give up every moment, every half hour to the twins. I tell John, 'I am not going to speak to you for a fortnight', when they come. I know I have to guard against this overpossessiveness, but every moment of their holiday is precious to me.

The experiment of us all living together has been erased from our general conversation. If ever I do bring up the subject, John dismisses it with, 'Darling, that didn't work. You are not strong enough.' That is the way it is explained away. I am not strong enough. But I know now that the reason for my fatigue was that I felt I had failed as a mother. I will add that when children have been largely disciplined by someone else, you don't find it easy to get a grip on them. You never catch up with those missed years.

JOHN: The whole experience of divorce and remarriage changed her, mellowed her. Partly because of her religious background she was always extremely intolerant of broken marriages or of parents whose behaviour was less than ideal. Nowadays, she takes a much more tolerant view and realizes that in the majority of cases there is something to be said on both sides, and that family disasters are frequently as much due to sheer foolishness or ignorance as malevolence. As far as the electric-shock treatment is concerned, the effects have slowed her down a bit, which is no bad thing in her case.

She puts so much of herself into whatever she is doing –

this has been her making and her undoing. When we first got married she kept on with her job, working at it on a part-time basis because we needed the money. The part-time compromise didn't really work out satisfactorily. Her boss, Ackpool, was a very trying, rude man. When I came home in the evenings it was nothing unusual for me to find her on the verge of tears or in tears. One evening, it was too much. I said 'I'm sick of having Ackpool every night. Let's give it up.' And she did.

In a way my reaction boiled down to self-interest, but I work extremely hard myself, and my hope that some interest would be shown in what I was doing was rarely fulfilled.

I am torn between wanting a Chinese wife who is always there with my slippers put out and bowing and scraping when I come in, and needing a person of equal intelligence with whom I can discuss matters.

LOUISE: I'm nearly forty-one and I've burnt myself out. From my early twenties onwards I held down what was virtually a man's job and I kept on working through marriage and pregnancies until just before Didi was born. My ex-secretary told me that my record was absolutely phenomenal. The work I could get through! Nowadays I have only to think of what I used to do and I want to go and lie down.

I could I suppose go back to my old job, but I wouldn't think of it. I have lost my taste and my nerve for work. I don't burn after being anyone exceptional now.

I now do comfortably in a week what I once hared through in a day. I like to be free to take Didi on a picnic when the weather is fine. I would just as soon that people admired me for being a good cook as for having a successful career. Besides, I've had a career.

JOHN: When Louise goes away, which is rare, I have a sense of incompleteness. I enjoy the married state and I feel comfortable and at ease when my wife is around. I don't sleep as well on my own. I like a double bed, I'm not talking about sex but about the cosiness and intimacy of the married relationship.

I am overjoyed by my daughter. The special satisfaction of being the father of a daughter is the contrast and similarity to yourself. The unwritten love affair is a tremendous thrill.

The longer Louise and I are married, the more predictable every gesture becomes. Sometimes I barely need to finish a sentence, we have become so intuitive about what the other is going to say next. It is very reassuring in some ways but as a man I think I miss an element of mystery. I would like to come home one evening to find Louise looking rather glamorous, steeped in scent and ready to seduce me. But this, alas, never happens in a long-standing marriage because practical issues tend to intervene – there is the central heating to be seen to, or whatever.

Moods are so hard to synchronize in a domestic set-up. Suppose I want to make love to her after dinner and then we say we must watch this television programme. She will probably go to bed first and she is asleep by the time I get there.

LOUISE: When he comes home he likes me calm and purring like a pussy cat with his slippers put out at a quarter to seven, the ice ready and the drinks arranged. He likes me calm, cool and collected and preferably having read a good book in the afternoon.

If ever I am unhappy it is because of frustration over the twins, or money, or general fatigue. But I never feel I want a lover or that I need anyone else, ever. I don't long to go to parties, as I did during my first marriage, in the hope of meeting someone else. That is worth a lot.

Mary

The Situation. An unmaternal mother who is deeply involved in her career assesses her reactions to the demands of parenthood. She has been married for five years and has two children aged nearly two and twelve months.

The Wife. Mary, aged twenty-seven, a librarian. She is married to Brian, in his early thirties, who is a dental practitioner.

The Place. A semi-detached house in Wandsworth.

MARY: I'm not in the least maternal but my husband is very paternal – he even loves babies. What made a huge difference to him was being there when our children were born; he felt involved. He hated it the first time because I was in agony and had a very difficult time. I was terribly afraid. You haven't a clue about what is going to happen and all the books play it down so much, saying so often that everything will be perfectly normal that you are convinced that, my God, it won't be.

We read one particular book which had a chart of emergency instructions for fathers about how to put your cigarette out if you are smoking, and to wash your hands and all these sort of clean actions. Brian learned it off by heart and knew the form so well that he was dying for me to have an emergency which he could handle. Probably, in the end, he was glad I didn't. But I was confident in him.

At hospital during the birth they let him be with me all the time, and for the actual delivery he was there with the gas and whatnot.

For all his good intentions and helpfulness he kept clapping the mask on my face just when I didn't need it, and taking it away at the moment when I did. But his ham-handedness made me feel more affectionate in a way.

A small, pink, ugly baby who does nothing but vomit and crap is not a very attractive prospect. There is nothing that a child who is so small can do that adds up to a response of any sort, and you have to get a response out of another human being to have any basis to work on at all. The advantage of bottle feeding, which I decided on to the tune of great reproaches from the hospital authorities, was that Brian could take it in turns with me, which made him feel he was sharing the burden. Not only that. The child showed its one and only response – which is to suck – to him. This thrilled me, the sight of it.

I don't want any more children. These two are reaching a stage where they are becoming human beings instead of sprawling trolls.

I detest the whole phase of pregnancy because this interferes with my ability to work, which is selfish but that is how I react. Some foul people romp through pregnancy all vitaminized and glowing, and I hate these people. I spend the first three months being sick, the second three months lying flat on my back, and the last three months so huge I can't move. A gross inconvenience, literally. I became so self-pitying that I thought I had precipitated my post-natal depression antenatally.

Our eldest child is nearly two, the other is nearly twelve months. I have had a daily girl to help with the children right from the start except for the first week home from hospital when I thought I ought to try to be a mother.

I realized as soon as I thought of employing somebody that there was a very strong chance that the children would prefer her to me, and think of her as Mummy.

When the girl first bathed the baby a great pang went through me, as might have been expected. I got over this very quickly indeed. I thought, at least she is doing the bathing.

But after that, I never felt jealous and oddly enough from the start the children knew she wasn't Mummy. The eldest child has only started to say Mummy and only said it to her father for a long time. But this doesn't worry me. They know.

As Brian's paternal feelings are so much stronger than my maternal ones I know it hurts him at times when I shriek at the children, and I do a bit. There is such an awkward gap between them that they do become unbearably tedious. At times I try to outscream them in hopes they will quieten down.

I know he wishes I wouldn't do it. But when he is left with them for a long time or when he has got to do anything for them other than playing – give them their tea or change the nappies – he begins to understand. He loathes the nappy business but he does it. And I am thankful that their father can be more naturally kind to them than I can.

Charles and Rosaleen Lemon

The Situation. The couple have been married for twenty-five years and they find that for the first time the house is empty of children. Their three children are away at universities. The couple are considering how best to rearrange their married lives in a way which will give a fuller life to the wife, yet take into account the final stages of protective parenthood.

The Husband. Charles Lemon, in his mid-fifties, has held the post of company secretary to a steamship company for fifteen years.

The Wife. Rosaleen Lemon, in her early fifties. She possesses no qualifications for employment other than secretarial. She is interested in music and painting.

The Place. An owner-occupied, semi-detached house in South London.

CHARLES: We had no children in the house for the first time in twenty-three years. It was rather peculiar and unusual. My wife was on her own during the day and she found time dragged. She just bustled around doing housework and she complained that when I went out in the morning she saw no one until I returned at night.

ROSALEEN: I got awfully fed up. I had been far too busy for the past twenty-three years to worry about taking a proper outside job. But when my last child left home to go to university I found myself living in a dead house.

I had always kept my hand in, and I'm grateful that I did. I did voluntary church work, I belonged to the Circle Trust which helps prisoners' wives, and for the past six years I did a one day a week secretarial job for pocket-money. But after six years of the same routine job, mostly copy-typing and filing, I began to feel I needed a sense of achievement.

My husband said that there was a chance of a job in the City near where he works. He said, 'Why not come with me, use the car and we will go together and come home together?'

CHARLES: I heard of this job employing temporary staff and I said to my wife, 'Why not give it a trial, it might be the answer to your problems?' It didn't mean committing herself to full-time work permanently. We looked upon the idea as an experiment.

I thought the journey might be too much for her, rush-hour travel is a bit of a strain.

ROSALEEN: I wasn't sure. This is the sort of pace you have got out of at my stage of life. You have to be prepared to stand in the tube. There is a terrific crush of people. But I thought I'd give it a try.

CHARLES: We now have morning tea upstairs in the bed-room, just before seven o'clock, and then I hop out and wash and shave and come downstairs and start the breakfast. I put a rasher on or some fish, make some toast and make some more tea. About eight o'clock we are ready to go off to the tube. We leave the car at the station, go by tube to the City. Then we have our coffee together, and sometimes do a crossword. We go our separate ways until we meet again at five-thirty for the return journey.

ROSALEEN: It was a big step for me. He has made it easier by getting me up in the morning and getting me going. It took me quite a time to get used to being up and ready to leave the house by eight o'clock. At home, you have so much freedom.

Before we leave in the morning I get the beds made and lay the supper, and we wash up breakfast. I pick up what we need for supper during the lunch-hour at work. Tonight we are having noodles and tomorrow an omelet. But I don't plan meals like I used to. The bulk of the shopping is done on Saturday morning and I get vegetables delivered.

CHARLES: When we get home in the evening it is a bit of a rush round. We don't have central heating so we have to get the fires lit, and some food cooked for supper. Anything urgent in the way of housework gets done at night. We often put a load in the washing-machine at night and get the ironing done.

ROSALEEN: I work mostly with a crowd of young Australian girls and they are a lot of fun. They tend to call me Mrs and everyone else by their Christian names but apart from that they don't make me feel too ancient.

During the lunch-hour I go to see the City churches or attend organ recitals, both terrific new interests.

CHARLES: She has shown me aspects of the City I hardly knew existed and I've worked there for twenty years.

When I discuss the experiment with people over lunch I add the fact that it is especially for her own benefit, and the primary object is to get her out of the house. It was that rather than the financial aspect. They accept that.

ROSALEEN: I ask myself, do I want to continue to work full-time on a permanent basis? At this stage, I simply don't know. There are so many sides to the question.

I wish I could train for a more interesting job. I took a secretarial course when I was young, but I have no professional qualifications, unlike my children. I recently tried to take a course in Adult Child Care but the nearest courses were held at Stevenage and as I can't drive I can't get there. So I didn't take the course. But in general there aren't nearly enough opportunities for the woman who is fifty upwards for training or retraining. If you dare say you are fifty you don't stand a chance.

A full-time job, whether it is routine or responsible, means I am away from the house during the day and my children are still at the stage when they like to come home for a break. When they come home, they like to find me there. This is what is so difficult to combine with any sort of full-time paid work.

This job I've got now is not too responsible and my employers don't mind if I disappear for a day or so occasionally. But even so it's a problem when one of the children elects to come back for more than a weekend.

A further factor is that the children do their holiday jobs from home. At Christmas two of them worked for the Post Office. In summer Roger was a park-keeper, Martin was a labourer and Cathy did the Adoption Society. On one long Vac. they got jobs working in a restaurant and Martin worked at BEA as a porter. They like a job with overtime.

I don't believe in pushing them out of the nest early and leaving them to sink or swim. I know they have got to be thrown out sometime, but they've got such a lot to stand up to.

CHARLES: Our house is too big and we think of selling it for a smaller place, perhaps nearer the City. But we are not entirely independent yet. We still have to provide accommodation for the children when they come home and we don't know where they are going to work. Any of them may work in London and they might want to live at home.

ROSALEEN: It is all new to us, dealing with grown-up children. Mostly, I think they need 'invisible' support, and will do until they all marry. They don't want to feel that they have got to worry about what is happening at home, but they want to be able to come back when it suits them. And when they do, I switch back to my old role of planning three square meals a day, baking cakes and being generally around the place.

We go up North mid-term to see them, taking a few extra pounds in cash. They all get a grant but we help out. Both the girl and the boys have got independent flats and they raided our house for electric fires, blankets, crockery, food and pictures. On average they write about once in ten days and ring up much more often.

CHARLES: The financial side of my wife's job isn't all that important and is likely to become less so. As from next year my tax position will change. My allowance for three dependent children will begin to be reduced as the children become financially independent, and the amount of my income tax will eventually be increased by £18 a month. With my wife's salary on top of that, the amount of tax to be paid on our joint income would hardly be an encouragement for her to work for money.

ROSALEEN: I earn £15 a week and at the moment it is worthwhile having. Anyway I would like to pay my way more. I contributed towards a twenty-first birthday party for Roger – we took the whole family out for a meal, and gave him a typewriter and money as a present and organized a terrific party.

We got a lot of gate-crashers. Saturday night is a bad night for party givers as the news spreads that there is a party on. But we had no fights, not that we ever have had.

My husband and I went out and left them all to it until twelve o'clock. Then we came back and got told off for trying to clear up so soon. It ended finally at two o'clock. A lot of them stayed the night, but I insisted that the boys slept downstairs and the girls upstairs.

CHARLES: They do tend to cling to one another. I think it is the noise that gets you down. The house is uncomfortably crowded and the mess afterwards!

ROSALEEN: A lot of middle-class people value their property too much. They are so afraid of anything being spoilt. At the party a leg was broken off a table, some glasses broken which we had hired, and some beer was spilt. That was the total damage.

Roger wrote us a lovely thank-you letter and we had a number of very nice thank-you letters from the boys and girls. They are a charming crowd, really.

CHARLES: We breathe a sigh of relief sometimes, now the

family has grown up. The children are all close together and the years when they were small was really a hard grind.

I'm closer to the boys than to my daughter, perhaps because we have a common interest in sport. Basically, I have more shared interests with my daughter, literature and music, but we don't discuss these things together.

At the moment our political views don't coincide. They are all to the Left, so we don't argue politics. Also, they consider my liking for Wagner and the Brontës rather square and crackpot.

However, they always bring plenty of life into the house.

ROSALEEN: I think he would like them not to be at home so much. He feels they should stand on their own feet now and that we are entitled to our own life a bit. After all, we have both given them a good many years.

There is more companionship for us, now. We go to the Festival Hall for a meal and a concert and it's nice not to feel that I've got to rush back to cook a meal for the family.

CHARLES: My wife has adapted to this new life very well. Someone we met the other day remarked that she was looking much better than when they had seen her previously – much livelier.

ROSALEEN: If the job doesn't work out I may start to study, I'd like that instead. I should enjoy reading literature and the classics. Children like to know you are there at home, and they like to ring up and they like to be able to come home. And in a way I think we should let them.

Glenda

The Situation. The wife needs to maintain close physical and emotional contact with her three young children, as well as fitting in her own creative work. The couple have been married for eight years.

The Wife. Glenda, aged thirty, an arts-school graduate who works on a part-time basis as a dress designer for firms supplying London and provincial dress boutiques. She is married to a civil servant in his early forties.

The Place. A flat in Chalk Farm, London.

GLENDA: I wouldn't say my marriage was perfect, it is full of friction and flaws. Most of my life is absolutely frightful, and I feel miserable, tired and fed up. But at the same time I feel it is worthwhile. Most people don't even have that.

In the daytime, I am very much a wife and mother. I feel I am the only person in the world who is capable of dealing with my children. I get very irritated with them, but they are only small for such a little while. Surely they like me being irritable with them all day. They get to know me and it brings us together when by bedtime I say, 'What an awful day and how difficult you've been.' For some reason they think that's fair. Whereas if you come in all smiles and sunny good temper at four o'clock they, in some way, resent it.

I know that if I let myself stray in my interests I would grow to resent the children, and I can't afford to let myself stray that far. Then it really would be a grind to have to look after three children that one didn't really care about. If you can't do it through real commitment then you can't do it through a sense of duty.

I would hate to have a full-time, proper posh nanny. My domestic habits are so appalling I couldn't bear her to see what went on in my house, the kind of things I eat and the way I wash up. Also, I like my children to feel that I am the person who does the dirty work. There is nothing like doing the dirty work for making you care for them, let alone making them care for you.

My dilemma is, do I have living-in help and work, or live without help and try to squeeze my own work in? It would be economical for me to go out to work full time but the strain of it would kill me.

I hate having girls around in the house because I am stuck with them in the evening, whether I like it or not, and so much depends on their daytime presence. Usually I start to work. My ideal working stretch is after the children have been put to bed at quarter past seven until about nine o'clock – my husband usually works late. I can get quite a lot done in that time. But this last girl who has just left us – much to my relief – is an unmarried mother, and had no kind of independence. As I felt mean about leaving her on her own I sat talking rubbish and watching 'Emergency Ward Ten'. Ridiculous.

An uncongenial au pair girl is a tremendous source of friction between husband and wife. My husband will complain, 'She's put a whole pot of cream in the trifle and anyway I hate trifle.' I will say, 'Well, she's only trying to do her best.' But I will be furious as well about this cream being poured all over the trifle in a pointless way. Then I will defend her, and we will have a row. We are both furious with her, but what we do is take it out on each other.

I find it very difficult to work at home because I can hear all the noises and when the children fall off chairs I want to run down. I have been trying to get out of the house to get to the factories three times a week, but in order to do that I have to employ two girls, a daily girl as well as a living-in girl. I really couldn't leave all three of them with one untrained person.

The arrangement did work for a few months, and to begin with the children didn't mind at all when I went out. Then we changed girls and there was a certain amount of trouble as they didn't care much for the replacement and they began to cry.

My husband is a great admirer of my work in an academic way, but if we didn't have the children we would drift more and more apart. I would have more time to spend designing and it is the whole design and fashion world which he doesn't like and considers unimportant. He is not interested in it.

I can hardly conceive that we would have any relationship

without the children. It is a great bond, admiration for one's offspring, and a very great point of contact, a man having a share in his children. I feel so much for the children. It is very nice to know that there is somebody in the world who doesn't think I'm an absolute fool for being so fond of them. He was always very polite about our babies and on my side about them being nice.

Sometimes during the day I have fits of complete moroseness when I'm convinced something has gone wrong with my work. Sometimes I have moments of euphoria when I'm washing up and the children are playing outside and everything clicks into place and I rush out and hug them, 'Oh, what wonderful children you are.' I am very temperamental. But you can't be too sentimental with children because you always have to change the nappies.

In marriage, the idea of freedom and not thinking about the other person is wonderful but it just never works out like that. I don't think you can be free with three children. It is as basic as that. I can't leave the house. My husband is technically freer than me because he can go to the pub if he wants to. But he doesn't want to, and he doesn't go, so nobody is free in our house. We are all stuck. The idea of being free in a spiritual sense appeals to me very much. But in the practical sense it is meaningless.

I don't know any really happy marriages but it seems to me that we are getting quite a lot out of our marriage. At least I know what I want to do, and my husband knows what he wants to do, and we try to do it, and we both enjoy the children.

What we are not getting we are too busy to miss. I really would hate a great empty gap, one does know people like that.

3. The sex imperative

Jo and Polly

The Situation. A young couple, both in the grip of disturbing emotional conflicts, attempt to find a mutual cure in the condition of marriage.

The Husband. Jo, in his late twenties, is bisexual. He comes from a working-class family background and is an art-school graduate employed as a graphic designer.

The Wife. Polly, in her early twenties, comes from a cultured family of Orthodox Jews living in the Midlands. She was educated at a girls' private boarding school and then went to university. Since adolescence she has suffered from suicidal tendencies.

The Place. A two-roomed flatlet in Gunnersbury Park.

POLLY: I asked Jo whether he wanted to marry me or not. He couldn't give me an answer but I guessed it would be yes. Then one evening we went and sat in a pub in a little country place and we talked and talked for hours about all the difficulties and I persuaded him there weren't any. The next morning we told our parents we were engaged practically. My parents didn't believe it. They took the view unless you have got a ring on your finger – and Jo couldn't afford a ring – you aren't engaged. They wouldn't accept it and they wouldn't tell anyone and my father wouldn't let me put an announcement in the paper because he didn't want his name associated.

My parents were absolutely dead against my marrying Jo. My family are well-known members of the Jewish community and Jo is not a Jew.

I admire my parents, especially my father, who is an exceptionally cultured and knowledgeable man. Indeed, I am probably a typical psychiatric case of being closer to my father than my mother – my mother has always upset me. She is a perfectionist and as chairman of countless committees she is always organizing other people's lives.

I have always wanted to escape from the inflexibility of my background. It is a hothouse in which people are very aware of each other's achievements in all forms. Leading a hard-working life, being honest, and having a purpose and being religious is all part of it. Culturally and intellectually our family life was stimulating, but at the same time I could not stand the limitation set upon my social freedom. I could not tolerate the idea that I was supposed to go out with some people, and not with others. I remain Jewish as opposed to any other religion, but I don't go to synagogue.

I had already given notice to the registry office, so technically we had a clear three months in which to get married at about ten minutes' notice.

I told my parents 'Please don't argue with me but I may come home tomorrow and say that I am married.' So we woke up on the Tuesday morning and we said 'are we getting married today?' Jo woke up earlier than usual, he's normally very difficult to get up in the mornings, and we said 'yes'. We telephoned our witnesses and got them together, and rushed out and bought Jo a shirt and me a hat and a magnum of champagne and checked with the Registrar. We turned up at the Registry Office two minutes early, waited for our witnesses, did it all and we couldn't really believe that this was all happening.

We took lots of photographs of the magnum, had a chocolate cake for lunch as we had no money left for a proper meal, which my parents thought was a huge joke. I telephoned my mother but I was too frightened to talk to her, Jo spoke first and she was full of congratulations, and we went round to see her. She offered to pay for our honeymoon. A super day.

JO: Up to the moment when we decided to get married, all I wanted was for her to disappear. When I first met her I found her physically attractive – she is like a Dresden miniature, very small and perfectly formed – but that quickly wore off. She became desperately clinging and I found this too tedious for words. Then she made a suicide threat, and I was convinced of its seriousness. She found no purpose in life and had been drifting from one lover to the next. She didn't know what she wanted, the people she liked didn't like her, the people who liked her she didn't care for.

I am a weak person in some ways, and I allowed myself to get involved in a set of circumstances where marriage to her was the end result. I had become dependent on her financially and finances are one's life, or they seem to rule mine. I am a dreadful spendthrift and Polly had helped me out with various loans.

Marriage was in any case a tremendously difficult step for me, partly because I didn't want to be tied down, and partly because I have homosexual inclinations.

POLLY: I do need him very much. Until Jo came along I never felt I was capable of a long-term relationship with a man. I had become very promiscuous and I didn't know which way to turn. I don't think promiscuity comes naturally to most women, and when you have done it you realize it isn't much fun and the worries are enormous. Without human relationships I don't see any purpose in living, and the act of making love at least brings a few moments of release, of belonging to someone. Belonging is the word because it means you have a place.

All my other relationships with men had broken down, perhaps because I am the one who likes to do the chasing. I can't bear men chasing me unless I particularly want them in which case I have probably chased them first and they have run a mile before they have turned round. The pattern is masochistic, an anti-self thing, because you know you are destroying relationships with people by doing this.

Jo needs me, he will be happier with me in his life, and this knowledge gives me a purpose. If he disappeared I should go out of my mind, literally. In the past, I have been very near suicide. I have never fought the idea of suicide because in my case it is not a panic state of mind. With me it is a logical state, a weighed up decision, taken perhaps for the wrong reasons. I would be frightened to live without the thought of suicide. It is an open door. Admittedly it opens into nowhere, but at the same time you can turn away from the dark room you are in.

JO: I have always enjoyed heterosexual affairs and I believe that I am homosexual only by inclination and circumstance. To me, the idea of a relationship with a man is always more interesting than the actual situation. There is an element of frustration in homosexual liaisons, I feel I have to justify myself, which is absent from my affairs with girls.

Men do like to maintain a dominant role socially even if it is simply lying in bed while the wife gets breakfast. In homosexual relationships this means one very strong partner and one very weak and probably effeminate partner which I don't wish to be. Or it means taking an equal role, and equality is always a struggle and I am too lazy to try. With Polly, I find I naturally take the role of the dominant partner, at any rate to a degree which satisfies my ego. Polly always gets my breakfast!

I loved this boy Clive, very much, with a passionate intensity that you can't control when first you fall in love. Perhaps it is always the same with the first person you fall in love with. But he was impossible to live with, egoistic, and the affair broke up because it didn't work on the human level.

Now Polly and I really do get on, although we both admit we have loved other people more.

The homosexual experience has just one extra advantage for me. I think that the male body is the extreme form of human beauty. I get more aesthetic satisfaction, for example, from looking at a Renaissance statue of a nude male than from studying the most beautiful statue of a Diana. I share the conviction of many Greek and Renaissance sculptors that there is more to appreciate, more to sculpt, in the young male body. The flesh is hard and firm and there are diverse rippling muscles beneath the skin. Women, it is true, are subtle and soft and curved. But that may not be what you want. I find a unique tactile pleasure in a male body.

It is always a thrill for me to meet a handsome man, a sort of mutual admiration I suppose. But I don't like homosexuals as a social type, and I cannot admire the people who share my sexual tastes. I dislike their camp mannerisms, their overt feminism. Really, I primarily enjoy the visual act of looking at boys and this is inevitably coupled with a desire to express my admiration sexually. I don't care for the more perverted homosexual practices, a form of mutual masturbation is as far as I ever go.

Being with a woman, being with Polly, is for me much better, much nicer and fuller in every respect than my homosexual relationships. Sexually I am perfectly happy and satisfied. Sex is fun with her, as it is meant to be.

Orgasm is richer with a woman and the whole act of love-making, especially afterwards, although perhaps the ideal for me would be a heterosexual sex act whilst looking at a beautiful boy.

POLLY: The fact of his being a homosexual doesn't worry me at all from the moral point of view. The thing that does disturb me is venereal disease, as I have accepted that he may want to go off with boys.

Whether I would share him with someone is a question we have discussed. Threesomes on a permanent footing do sometimes work – but I don't think this will happen to us.

He is a marvellous lover. The proof was on Sunday. We had been a bit unromantic and rowed a bit for a few days, then we went off into the countryside for the day. We were sitting beside a cornfield miles away from anywhere and we decided to make love. It was my idea and we did, and I got my back almost bleeding which must prove something about his virility.

Jo is rather too beautiful for a man and this is one of the points my mother objected to. I thought he was gorgeous but she thought he was rather too gorgeous. This is certainly a reason why other men find him so attractive, but his body is very masculine. The only signs of physical effeminacy are the fine features of his face.

JO: I don't regard myself as an enormous problem. People today regard this that or the other common human experience as a capital letters P.R.O.B.L.E.M. But today so many personal situations need not be a problem.

POLLY: He is immature about money, terribly childish. I don't know how he will grow out of it – possibly with psychiatric treatment but that seems such a long way round. He always thinks he can spend what he earns at the end of the month, now. It is as simple as that. His debts are small but continual, which is worse. He will go out and do extravagant things. When you haven't got the money for a new shirt you should wear the ones you've got. What I'm worried about is having to ask my father for money which would mean he could lose respect for Jo.

Yet it is these differences between us that hold us together. His weaknesses make me feel strong. He is irresponsible and I am responsible and conscientious. He is slightly effeminate and I have a masculine side. He borrows things from people – I can't because I don't like being surrounded by things which aren't mine because I feel guilty about them.

I am respectable despite being promiscuous, which was my one lapse, and I am prudish – qualities I owe to my background and these I do not reject at all. I like a certain amount of respectability and so does Jo.

JO: Polly is impeccably middle-class, and so honest. I'm not dishonest but sometimes I let the bills pile up. Perhaps the difference in attitudes is really part of the difference between men and women. Women are more realistic, more sane. Polly would never – as I do – ring up the bank manager and ask him to pass a cheque for a restaurant bill when the money isn't there. Horror of debt is a typical middle-class virtue, but in this respect I am hoping to be able to hang on to my Bermondsey background and not worry too much about the overdraft.

In other ways though I feel I am gradually acquiring middle-class values. Someone remarked the other day that I speak much better than I used to, whatever that meant. I am careful about pronouncing words correctly and I try to speak grammatically which really I don't. My grammar is appalling and worse after a few gins.

POLLY: I laugh at Jo's efforts to put a smarter image on himself, but the middle-class label doesn't come into it. A class division indicates the outlook of a broad stratum of society, but today the social groups are much smaller. And again, artists have always been a class apart. Middle-class is much too broad a term to define the mixtures of attitudes and values which someone like Jo wishes to acquire. It is a mixture of what was good in the past and what is relevant in the present.

JO: Polly is my backbone. Her insistence on some kind of organization in my life is marvellous. I'd never get to the office on time if she didn't organize me.

When I come home in the evening I often pretend to be rather boorish. I come in through the door and say 'Hello' in a deliberately gruff manner. It is a sort of game, the antithesis of playing the beaming young husband role – a part in which I am hardly type-cast anyway. Sometimes I like playing games.

POLLY: He made the curtains, I didn't even choose the material. We have faint rows about it but these are issues I don't care about and usually he is right, so I let him have his way. I drive better than he does but he's not keen on my car. Firstly, it is not his car, and secondly it is in brown and white which he considers unaesthetic.

I have learnt a bit more tact than I had a year ago when I had none. On major decisions I try to convince him of the sense of my argument and leave it to him to decide.

Jo is very conscious of my appearance. He enjoys me because I am a small person, blonde and skinny. He has to be protective and already he feels more masculine. He tells me what sort of hairstyles suit me best and when I need more powder on my nose. He is very critical about my clothes and likes me to wear prettily boyish clothes. The other day I bought some new briefs with a straight line across the hips and he said, 'You look very boyish', and looked terribly pleased.

JO: Because she is so fragile physically she looks almost like my daughter. She is the antipathy of a mother figure to look at and is very different from my own mother. Judged by her looks she appears anti-bossy and undomineering. But in fact she is subtle and plays this role without appearing to.

POLLY: Marriage has made us feel more secure. We feel that things can go wrong and they will work out in time and it doesn't matter if you have a quarrel.

We are learning to live together, to accept each other's faults and failings. Personal little habits which I was ashamed of – I suck my thumb – which I don't normally let people see, become shared knowledge. I can be completely open and honest. I can tell him everything, anything. We counted up the other day how many affairs we had had, and we estimated that we had had about the same number of men.

JO: I haven't had a homosexual affair for over a year now, and I don't feel I need it. I think that with Polly's love and her way of accepting the situation I shall grow up out of my homosexual urges. It is very sound psychology on her part that she doesn't make a fuss about preventing me – she plays it as a bit of a joke. I'm not sure whether she hasn't consciously decided that a tolerant approach is the best antidote. If she were to scream and fuss and object I might pursue the idea merely as a reaction against the discipline.

Sometimes I think to myself that it might be fun to break out but when it came to the point I sense taboos would come into it. My marriage is based on a mutual trust. She says she won't have an affair with anyone else and she won't, she is so honest. And this gives me something to live up to.

POLLY: I'm four months pregnant and I'm not at all worried. I've been warned about the dangers as far as Jo's reactions are concerned. He'll probably go off me, and my case is complicated by the fact that I shan't be able to make love for two months or so before the baby is born. He may well take up with someone else. Jo told me, and I believe him, that he loves me too much to want another woman. But I take the view that if he is unfaithful with a boy, this is to be expected. He will never leave me for another man.

Being pregnant, I don't feel in the least suicidal any more. I don't think I could abandon life whatever happens now. Already I can even be alone without feeling lonely.

JO: I am tremendously pleased about the baby, and it presents me with a challenge. I want the satisfaction of proving everyone wrong about our cracking up under the strain of Polly's pregnancy. Admittedly, it is early days yet and Polly still retains her Dresden-like proportions. I have a habit of not seeing problems – I don't foresee any great rift.

Joan and Jack

The Situation. The marriage has survived twenty-four years of switchback phases on almost every level. The husband lives in the public eye and the wife's life is largely confined to home and family interests. The couple have four teenage children.

The Husband. Jack, in his late forties, a well-known figure in the communication business.

The Wife. Joan, in her mid-forties. At home, she helps her husband with some aspects of his work.

The Place. A country house and garden fifty miles away from London.

JACK: I feel as if I have been *endlessly* married. I got married when I was nearly twenty-one during the war in 1942. We had known each other for three weeks so the whole thing was pretty precipitous. I was in the Navy and at that time everything seemed imminently in danger of collapse and nothing seemed permanent so I suppose it was natural to rush into things. I wouldn't advise anyone to get married on this kind of basis, but oddly enough I think I would have married her in other circumstances. It is difficult to be sure about this. I had no intention of getting married and was not attracted to the idea of marriage in the least, but having met her, she was the only person I had encountered up till then who had any kind of empathy and who excited me mentally, intellectually. She's in her forties now and she's an attractive woman. She was very pretty. She has a gay and sparkling personality and is a very intelligent girl – she can argue and talk which I like. There's an element of suiting oneself in this, because the kind of life I intended to live would have been impossible with a dependent, clinging, passive woman. That couldn't have lasted. Although Joan has felt on many occasions that we lead a pretty shaky sort of life and pretty unsatisfactory, nevertheless she is a self-sufficient person with her own resources who is able to respond to this sort of challenge.

JOAN: We have had terrific crises and squabbles at various times but I'm astonished sometimes at how alive our marriage still is. To the extent that when we meet we have so much to talk about, it is always half past two or so before we go to bed really. We talk – the chit-chat obviously about the children and also the news of the day and his work. He is somewhat unpredictable and I have got to be alert and quick and ready to adjust to a mood or an idea. There are times when all the irritations well up. If he is in a bad mood he can be sharply critical, maybe something went wrong at work and he notices everything that's wrong like the cobweb over there or an unmended chair. But he always compliments me, always, if a meal is good. He will also remark on it if he thinks it wasn't good. He will also nearly always notice if I'm looking nice, if I've got a new dress on. My hair – the hair styles I can have are limited because he doesn't like me in a lot of the new styles – but again at least he does take notice. I regard this continuing interest in this aspect of me with astonishment. I keep wanting to know more about other people who have been married as long as we have to see if this aliveness obtains in other marriages. He phones me every day unless we have had a row – but we had a row before he left this week so he hasn't rung for three days.

JACK: In the kind of life I live, one is subject to many temptations and nobody is more easily tempted than I am. All along this has been a grave difficulty. The trouble is I love girls. There are a number of things here – one is having a name that people have heard of. If I wished I could live a very promiscuous life indeed, in that there are no problems if my inclinations were to sleep around constantly. Girls are endlessly available. I am not particularly attracted to an orgy of promiscuity but nevertheless problems do arise and not infrequently. Twice my marriage teetered on the brink of breaking-up which was because of other girls. There was one girl whom I wanted to marry, the other I didn't, but I was desperately involved with her. Both these situations were known to my wife and therefore both periods were a very unhappy time for her. I am glad neither happened. In the case of the one I really was in love with, she wouldn't, she was Catholic. We lived together for a time and in the end it dispersed, which I am relieved about now as it would never have worked. She is the sort of girl who would have driven me mad in the end. Although my life is a very untidy one, I am fanatical about surface organization – I need things to be run properly around me – I need tidy desks and I can't bear squalid littered houses. This girl led a totally chaotic life and it would have driven me insane. I was crazy about her for a year or so. But since then nothing comparable has happened and in fact I would never again wish it to. I have made absolutely unwarrantable demands upon my marriage. I am tremendously fond of my wife and I respect her very much and admire her and enjoy being with her, but I've always been faced with the difficulty that the delights of sexual alliance inevitably fade in a long-term relationship.

JOAN: When people have been married as we have for twenty-four years I think sex usually becomes spasmodic or very routine. When he comes home, even if we don't make love, it's comforting to get into bed and really hug one another. There is a great feeling of warmth because we haven't been in bed together for a week anyway. I think there is something to be said for this kind of physical closeness even if sex is no longer as thrilling as it used to be.

JACK: There are several girls with whom I have had long-term erotic friendships whom I see frequently, and I enjoy doing this. I don't make any demands on them of total fidelity or commitment, because I don't really want that. The worst times Joan and I have had are when she has made heavy demands upon me and my reaction has always been to resist these demands and to fight them. I suppose if I had acted with more premeditation, I could have saved half the heart-burning and misery but I don't react in that way. When she told me to give up the girl my reaction to this was bitter hatred of being pushed into a situation of being made to act in a certain way, which precipitated disaster upon disaster, getting worse all the time.

The situation now is an unwritten compact – I try, and I

think most of the time succeed – in never allowing any of these other relationships to impinge upon her at her expense. If she is coming up to London and has changed it from Tuesday to Wednesday and I have made a private arrangement, I cancel it. I have insulted her in the past and unforgivably and this I try not to do any more. On these two particular occasions I treated my wife abominably in that I neglected her and abandoned her interests altogether, in favour of these other girls. I've tried to reform since then.

I feel that if I was bound entirely within my marriage that it would not have lasted. I would have exploded and gone. In a curious way, the fact that I have been able to have love affairs and friendships and to meet other girls has preserved my marriage because without this I don't think I would have been able to contain myself within the inevitable limitations of marriage. What has always been exciting for me is meeting new people. I know I am a terribly immature person and as I have continued in this boyish vein, freedom has made the marriage viable. This unspoken agreement is never discussed.

My wife, I am quite sure, knows that when I am absent from her I am seeing other people, there are never questions about this. Her only demand being, which is an implicit demand, that I am not neglectful which I think is tremendous of her.

I do love her and cherish her and would not again betray her in the sense of making her suffer. This is the thing – the diminishing of people and their feeling of loss of love and loss of security. Another issue – what she finds deeply upsetting is that mutual friends are talking about the fact that I am having an affair with someone else and she gets knowledge of this when she appears in London and comes to parties. So again I try not to bring this upon her.

JOAN: In general, I don't want to know the details of his affairs. I always know when he has a new girl anyway without being told directly. His attitude towards me changes, he rejects me and becomes very difficult and moody at home. But in the rare cases where he is seriously emotionally involved I do need to know what is going on. I like to know what it is that I'm facing.

Men don't realize. They imagine that the way you think about them doesn't change. But the kind of married life my husband leads inevitably brings in its wake a succession of lies and falsehoods which eventually I discover. Years of it must change your estimation of the man's character. At one time, I used to admire him for his honesty. I still admire many aspects of him, his enthusiasm for living, his intellectual honesty – he can still get angry about public and political acts which we both consider to be immoral, and I respect him for his conscientious approach towards his work. But I cannot admire him for his selfishness and his disloyalty towards me.

I am not solely concerned in this matter about my own position. I resent, on his behalf, the way in which his behaviour exposes him to malicious giggles, to the fact that our friends can make snide cracks at his expense. The sort of thing I mean is this; when he and I are together with friends and there is a pretty girl around who may be about our daughter's age, the remark has been made to me, 'I don't think she is quite young enough for Jack', and it really makes me feel sick. If they are prepared to make the remark in my presence then I know they must be making these cracks in front of anybody and everybody. He puts himself in a position whereby he is diminished in this way.

Periodically throughout my marriage I feel that if I don't get out of this I shall die. I get moments when I just hate them all. I think bloody awful children and lousy man, but it might last a couple of days, it might last for a week. When I am having difficulties, having Jack problems, money problems or children problems, the worst thing is that they belong to both of us. If you're married and go out with somebody else for that evening you can forget about your worries. But since our problems are joint problems we can't be together and forget ourselves for an evening.

JACK: I know that she has had several affairs but nothing of any length or consequence. Usually it is a transitory thing when she has been away. It's a fearfully masculine excuse and rationalization but it is biologically true to say that the sexes act differently. Man is a pursuer, a hunter and essentially girls want stability and a home and young. I don't think most girls really want to dodge around. Late teens early twenties certainly, but then they prefer to settle for some kind of home. By the nature of her situation, a woman has a home to look after and she is stuck.

JOAN: It is much more difficult for a woman to have an affair within marriage. You might meet someone you liked, he might ask you out, you accept and maybe go to bed with him. Then one of the children gets measles, or his next free day coincides with half-term arrangements, and on it goes like this for week after week. There isn't time for a real affair to develop and eventually you begin to wonder what the original attraction was.

My husband for example, is free to make his own private arrangements. He can come home in the evening or stay up in our flat in London. Sometimes he doesn't let me know that he is coming home until the end of the day, and then of course, he expects to see me. It is very difficult to make plans of your own in these circumstances.

Another point of difference between the sexes in this matter is that like many women, I do not necessarily have to go to bed with a man in order to have my femininity confirmed. It is enough to know that someone finds me attractive enough to ask me out. I don't even need to accept. But unless a man actually goes to bed with a girl he doesn't feel that he has won.

I like being by myself but not all the time. I think this is the point. I like being in the country if I can go to London sometimes. And sometimes if I haven't been to London for, say, a fortnight I think I must go to London, I shall go nuts, how can I bear it down here and I go to London and I think what on earth did I get fussed about? But just having got away I recover.

JACK: Last year I had to go to Hollywood on a production deal and I spent part of the summer driving round the West Coast with her. I found this very happy and enjoyable and relaxed. I enjoy being with her and its tremendously nice when we have a prolonged phase of togetherness – just talking, which we seldom get the chance to. At the weekend at home there is a great pile of absolutely cursory, unimportant oddments that take up most of the time we can spend together.

JOAN: I think one of the reasons our marriage is so alive is that it has been very much an up and down relationship. It hasn't been awful for ages but there have been times when I have been critically unhappy. And then there have been times when it's been absolutely swinging. But I can't stand it being all so sweet for so long. I feel I've just got to have a quarrel. I can't stand evenness. I find real togetherness absolutely suffocating. I like to have lots of people being around the place but I also must have some time to myself.

In marriage, you've got to learn to grow together again. The quarrels that have got to be had because the resentment has to be exorcized, spoken and disposed of, have got to be mended. Married life is made up of ebb and flow, good patches and bad patches, feeling that life's marvellous and feeling that life is terrible. In ordinary everyday living, sometimes I feel happy and sometimes I don't.

JACK: I think I have changed quite a lot in the last few years and I no longer feel the compulsion to be so feverishly active. I think perhaps I could settle for something entirely different and quieter, more sensible, now.

Frances

The Situation. An emancipated girl, highly conscious of her own sexuality, marries. Her reactions are complex and ambivalent – part feminine, part anti. She has been married for two and a half years and is the mother of children aged nearly two and twelve months.

The Wife. Frances, in her late twenties, a freelance computer programmer script writer. She is married to Tom, in his early thirties, who is a businessman.

The Place. An Edwardian terrace house and garden on a short mortgage, in Twickenham.

FRANCES: I had all the same sort of desires as every other girl to get married. Marriage is the mark of acceptability; somebody finds you splendid enough to be the only person worth spending their life with, and so forth.

When Tom did ask me to marry him I admit that I probably grasped at the opportunity. I wasn't sure what I was marrying. I knew that he was a person who was much more understanding and sensible and calm than other various passionate and unbalanced people I had come across. So I married in the cool.

He is much more influenced by my moods than I am by his, which sounds the wrong way round. But he is, because he takes his responsibilities so seriously. He feels he should be responsible for my state of happiness and if I'm not bubbling and gleeful and ha ha! he thinks there is something wrong with *him*. Everything that is wrong with me he immediately attributes to himself. Strikes me as being rather vain as well as responsible.

We bought a house and moved out a bit because of the children. I didn't know anybody at all in the neighbourhood and was fairly inaccessible stuck at home with the babies and working. I had no office contact so I hadn't got the normal run of friends one has in an office. But because I was working all the time at home I didn't have the typical mother's play-group contacts and coffee mornings and all that dreary stuff, but nevertheless people.

I was fit prey. Somebody I knew came around, a married friend of mine, and said he had problems to talk about. I was curious and delighted. Except of course it ended up with this last sentence of 'I'm in love with you'.

To my credit perhaps this came as an absolute, total shock. I hardly knew him. There had never been any wink-wink thing going on at all. The whole episode became messy and stupid. Because I was on my own, I suppose I had thought, poor thing, and let myself be too sympathetic and consequently got lumbered.

When you are married you don't stop needing the normal, everyday, slightly flirtatious but harmless contacts you have with men. But men either think that you are not there to be *had* anymore – even if having you was the last consideration in their minds when they used to know you. Or, she is all tucked-up and happy and who am I to break in? They don't need people dropping in anymore.

When Tom is away what I do frequently want, and I admit this, is a quick screw. But everybody, of course, expects me to be feminine, and want to get involved thereafter. I don't. I'm like a man about this. I need a screw every so often and like to have it and get it over with and cheerio. But since men don't expect a woman to feel like this, you can't. You get yourself horribly tied up. So I masturbate. This serves.

If I had not been pregnant for all the short two and a half years of my marriage, perhaps I would have wanted a great deal more variety in my sexual experience. I tried valiantly to carry on with my sex life as far as I could until each of my two children were born, and as quickly as I could thereafter. But I was a physical mess, and this made it difficult and painful, and I really did my duty and let my husband have his fill. I was still able to achieve orgasm but sex itself lost a lot of its titillating side.

Tom is perhaps the most out-and-out puritan to be found. This is because he has so many violent and unpleasant sexual impulses all raging around in his mind that he decided years ago to exercise a fierce self-control. He succeeded so well that his discipline has become oppressive and fearsome in some ways. He is sexually a very able man, but he is straightforward about it. No little incidental thrills or elaborate sexual fantasies.

I don't find sex difficult, and when I'm not pregnant or recovering from a pregnancy I can get as much enjoyment out of it as I want to. Like most people I have fantasies and like most people I find the fantasies look fatuous in reality. You can't expect a man to do the sort of things your nether minds conceive and not see him as an absolute idiot. In imaginative fantasy, dignity is somehow always maintained. But if someone chased me round in boots with a whip, which is not what I want but if it were, I would be so reduced to giggles that all the excitement would die. I have in fact had affairs before marriage which were more interesting in a complex sexual way, but so what? In the end I got far less satisfaction out of it. If I go to bed what I'm after for Christ's sake is an orgasm, and the more the better, and if there is a simple way of doing it, all right.

When Tom and I began courting I had come out of an affair, and with this man I had shown a lot of non-restraint which to Tom represented itself as passion and in fact was mere foolish behaviour. But to Tom this was an aspect of myself which I had not revealed to him and he felt jealous about it. Maybe he wanted to stir me up.

When we were married he had the most terrible nightmares about this man and would frequently get up in the middle of the night and walk out of the house and go for long walks. On a couple of occasions he woke up hitting me because of his dreams. I thought the obsession would go immediately I had a baby. But he had this mania which was absolutely untrue and very unfair – that the child might be the other man's. But now it has been forgotten and we can actually joke about it. He is a passionately jealous man and humiliating as it is to admit I think that probably the power of his jealousy holds me more in rein than anything else. I know the destruction it could bring about.

I still have this corny conviction that you have got to look lovely for your husband. Good heavens, when I wave good-bye to him, he goes off to a sea full of lush secretaries. You must show some sense of responsibility in this respect – I take about three quarters of an hour in the morning to get dressed and made up and hair and everything.

I think how mean it is that his secretary should see so much more of him than I do and also that she should see him in his restrained, refined mood. I see him as he really is, when I see him.

I look ghastly, vile, without my face on. He doesn't often see me without make-up, even in bed. He has this thing about my eye make-up and as a result it practically always stays on at night. I have a five minute washing session and on it goes again. After two and a half years of marriage, surely one would think I could do away with it? But I can't face my own face and I don't see why he should have to. You go to bed at night, and this is the only time you have for the romantic thing and then he sees it all stripped off. What's left is so unromantic and unsexy, why should he want it? Besides I feel that I'm no longer attractive in anything but the most super-ficial way because I feel very much marked by childbirth. My stomach doesn't bear inspection.

Adrian

The Situation. A husband with ambivalent emotional and sexual attitudes parts from his wife after seven years of marriage. They have a son of five years who is in the wife's care.

The Husband. Adrian, in his early thirties. He is a painter and a poet whose work is known to a growing and critically receptive audience. He had known and admired the woman whom he married since boyhood.

The Place. Adrian's bachelor flat in Battersea, London.

ADRIAN: There was constantly this battle for power between us, in which both of us used the most underhand psychological methods. She is, I suppose, a very formidable woman, very forthright and strong-minded with a very clear idea of life – of right and wrong – and in fact quite masculine and dominant. I also was quite strong-minded and felt that all the most profound decisions had to be made by me in the end and resented her taking this masculine role, very much.

I like everything in the place where I leave it – in fact I tend to be a tyrant about this. A room has to be visually right for me and our drawing-room upsets me particularly because it was not my taste at all. The colour of the carpet is all wrong. I don't look at it any longer. Things like food and drink – coffee especially – must be exactly right. So this is rather a bore for a woman, if she doesn't feel the same way. I am a much better cook than she. Much. She could hardly cook at all before our marriage. She lived on boiled eggs and baked beans.

The crux of the problem is partly that we were both symbols to each other as something else and we both loved what we thought the other was. She personified to me complete security in an intellectual, spiritual form and absolute sanity away from the chaos and confusion of the world. In fact the trouble was I worshipped her and always have done – I met her when I was first a boy of fifteen and she was seventeen – and I think it was then that this relationship of worshipper and idol got fixed. She used to behave like a goddess and order what one could do and what one couldn't. The whole reality of her is completely clouded by this ten years of worship, and the fact that she went to Oxford and I never did, it's all part of it.

I married seven years ago when I was twenty-seven and she was two years older. We thought we were in love with each other – the usual thing. She saw me as the great talented artist who would show her the truth which intellectual curiosity hadn't – I mean the study of history and politics and so on. She thought there was some hidden truth in art which my instinct would uncover. In fact the happiest moments of our marriage were probably when I had finished a new painting, and would bring it in from the studio and she would be so excited and stimulated by having something new which before was nothing. This kind of aesthetic communication we always had and still have. She's still very interested in what I do.

When we got married she was engaged in research and I had to live near her in a dreary little provincial town. This depressed me like mad because I had lived there for nearly five years and this caused enormous trouble because I found it so unbearable. The train service to London was so bad and I couldn't get to theatres or see my friends easily. And then we had the child pretty quickly – about eighteen months after we got married. She got terribly hysterical in her pregnancy, and vast, really vast, and the baby was late – five weeks late. We thought it was never going to come.

Sexually I discovered something very odd, that I couldn't sleep with her after she was about four or five months gone, because it seemed almost incestuous. It was a strange thing. Aesthetically I loved to look at this swollen stomach – but actually it repelled my emotions. It was so vivid – my child growing there – that to approach near it seemed obscene. And then she had a terrible, terrible childbirth that went on for forty-eight hours, it was awful and traumatic for her.

And immediately after that she had that very common thing – depression – and it went on for about six months and she had to have drugs for it. The point was that she couldn't do much because she lost all drive. She couldn't work any longer. She got very fat, and would just sit and smoke and drink tea. So this didn't help very much and I had to take over a lot of baby minding – nappies, the lot. Mind you, I quite enjoyed this kind of thing really because I was dotty about the baby. She eventually came out of that phase. The other major problem was at that period everything depended on my income alone, as a writer and painter. Then it was literally about £650 a year, which was crucial with the three of us to live off it.

She looked on me as an irresponsible playboy, as well as being a serious artist, whose opinions intellectually certainly weren't to be considered very seriously. She said that she never respected me at all. Though she loved me, and she still sometimes now says she loves me, she didn't ever like me very much. So this is very odd, you don't either like or respect your husband, but think you love him. That is bound to cause great psychological disturbances.

I enjoyed going to bed with her but only up to a point. I like to be quite adventurous and loose myself and such small things as, let us say to begin with, tenderly biting flesh. With her this was right out – it's something I've always liked doing and most women seem to have enjoyed it. She'd get furious about this. This is because I discovered she had and still has an almost hysterical hatred of losing control of her body. If you picked her up and she wasn't touching the floor, she'd become hysterical, and so the least pain like that, she would feel she had no control over her own body. She wasn't master of it and this one fact did make her quite wild. So in fact love-making was all right but it had to be pretty conservative, and once you know there is a barrier you tend to get a bit bored. She had orgasms, as she would feel that this was within her control, but she could choose *not* to have one.

Then I did become unfaithful and felt terribly guilty, and she wasn't unfaithful – partly because sexually she's not particularly attractive and really never got the offers. She tended to be and still is rather plain. Let's face it, this is partly the fact why people don't go to bed – they can give moral reasons for their behaviour but if they don't get the opportunity, this must partly account for their restraint.

One of the first things is for both partners to be equal in the sense that they are both equally physically attractive. It doesn't matter if a husband is plainer than a wife because it never matters with men, but if the wife is a lot plainer than her husband it can cause enormous twisted jealousy. But they also have to be equal, I think, in intelligence and in generosity of nature too, because if you have one person who has really a meaner nature than the other, then you get all sorts of difficulties developing. One partner is always wanting to give himself to the rest of society far more than to the other partner, and then the wife thinks 'he loves everybody else except me.' And then of course you must be bloody certain that you do love the person. So many people believe that love exists when they only need the partner for some psychological fulfilment. And it isn't love at all. One has to be extremely cautious about this, about your own reasons for loving.

The amount of guilt I felt about being unfaithful, even if it was only say two or three times a year, just got bigger and bigger. I am old-fashioned in this way, I do believe that sex belongs to love. I believed it all depends what your wife is like, but with her the only possibility of a happy marriage was to be faithful. And after two years I lacked this. I knew she had partly driven me to this, in all sorts of odd ways, and she knew it as well. In the end I had to be truthful and the truth had to come out and we did talk about it, and I said I'd try again and she affected that it was partly her fault.

Strangely enough when we got away, abroad, and had holidays without the child, we had wonderful, happy times. Because she always felt a deep sense of responsibility and when she was at home she was a mother first to her child and the husband didn't really come into it at all. She wasn't a wife.

But once she was away – we went away twice without the child to Greece and Vienna – she became like a lover in all the romantic ways and was sweet, charming and we had lots of sex and it was all right.

The final straw really was that we were arguing in front of our son who was then four and a half years old, because he loved us both and he was being torn in half with devotion to us both. I could see that nothing would be more damaging to his psychology than to see his mother and father tearing each other apart and nothing could upset me more deeply.

She was a failure to me I suppose, but then I failed her as well. It was fifty-fifty. Our marriage became mostly hysterical rages. I would generally sit quiet, but after our rows had gone on for half an hour, I might throw something – not at her, at the wall. Then she would go into wails and sobs and hysteria because I was being violent. And she had been violent with words for about half an hour. I have no real regrets because I know I learnt so much – I learnt a lot about women. I learnt a lot about human beings and I could never regret it because of my son.

4. The money and work factor

Lily and Mac

The Situation. A working-class marriage pitched against the problems of poor housing conditions and an economic recession in the husband's trade. The couple have been married for five years and they have three children under five.

The Husband. Mac, in his late twenties. He was a seaman in the Navy, and is a skilled worker in the shop-fitting and decorating trade. He is at present on sick benefit.

The Wife. Lily, aged twenty-four. She left comprehensive school at sixteen and before her marriage worked as a women's hairdresser.

The Place. The couple's home – two rooms in cold water premises in a semi-detached near Wandsworth.

LILY: Some people are quite content to live on £13 a week and struggle along for years like it. I couldn't live like it, I couldn't. That's why I've got a job to help out. Mac's still on sick benefit. It's certainly not for want of trying. He went down to the doctor's last week to get a final certificate, and he said, no, he can't go back to work yet.

MAC: With me earning good money and then coming down to a low wage of £13, that's what put us in debt. Up till last year I was earning an average of £1,500 a year. But this has been a very bad year for me due to the slump, the tax and the bank squeeze.

It has taken me four years to pay off the debt on the three-piece suite – there is a settee to go with it but that is stuck in the bedroom because there isn't the space for it in here – nearly £100 that, a refrigerator and an electric cooker and television. I'd paid it all off on the television but we had to sell it at Christmas. The one we've got now is hired.

LILY: Mac used to earn good money when he was in exhibition work or shop-fitting, he used to get £35 a week or more sometimes. But they've tightened up on all the jobs. If he could get a good job he'd get one. It's just as simple as that. But there aren't any jobs going.

For months and months he used to come in from work, have his dinner and he would sit down in the chair and it would be figures all over the place. He was working out ways of trying to get money – the different jobs he could get and if he got them how much money he would be getting and what he would do with the money. He was like that for ever so long.

There is plenty of jobs going on the road at a low wage with £16 a week or something but that's ridiculous. You can't expect a family of five and a half to live on that.

MAC: The figuring was a question of mind occupation. I sold the television so there was no telly and the figuring kept me mind occupied. It's my place to get the money, see. It's up to me. I've always done the worrying with us and now food comes first, rent comes last – we owe one month's arrears and this month's rent – well, you've got to feed a young family, haven't you? If you are very weak you could go suicidal about it, but I don't class meself as very weak.

LILY: We had a couple of letters from the landlord. He writes very polite letters and threatened action. So I went out to work in an office. With my new job we are hoping to pay off the arrears soon. The landlord's been very good really, but Mac says he has to be.

With Mac off sick my money helps out with the regular payments. So we are not really all that much better off. We're not in pocket but once he gets back to work we will be.

MAC: The rent is £3 18s. 4d. for two rooms and a kitchen. The three kids are in one, and we sleep in the front room. £1 for the coal, £1 for the light, that's nearly £6. It cost me 10s. in bus fares to get to work. I give Lily £6 10s. for food, and she has 18s family allowance. We certainly don't have any spare, as when I'm working there are weeks I'm only bringing home £13.

LILY: What I intend doing with my money if it's possible – I get £10 a week for a five day week – is some towards the rent arrears, some shoes for myself and then some clothes for the children – socks, pants they need.

I shall keep on with the job because I enjoy it. I'd fight if I had to give it up. It gives me a break from the children, it gives them a break from me, shouting at them all the time. I'll be a better person for it. We'll need to save a bit. My money will go into the bank just the same as his does. It's combined money to us, not his or mine.

MAC: I was off sick for eight weeks at the beginning of the year and I'm on sick benefit now. I lost two stone in weight earlier through this poison in the gums, pyorrhoea, picked up in the Navy. They took twenty-four teeth out in one go and I feel a lot better for it. They told me to wait a year, well it's nearly up, and I can get me false teeth when I've got the money. But you still have to pay a certain amount, £1 for a first visit I think and it is about £5 for the set. Then I had the mumps. The kid had the mumps first and then I got them. It's more severe in an adult, the swellings and that. It was very painful down below. I could hardly walk.

LILY: He can laugh! It was a lovely rest for me! But it was very unsettling about his teeth. I didn't know what to buy for him to eat from one week to the next. It was practically the same thing every day, soup and bread, soup and bread. He wouldn't touch a tin of baby food. The puddings are very nice, I told him. I used to finish them up myself with the babies. But he wouldn't touch a tin.

When he had the mumps I took a job as a cinema usherette in the evening. That was all right – it didn't start till 6.30 p.m. – so with a bit of luck I got the kids into bed before I went so my husband didn't have much trouble with them, because they play up with him. Usually they were all right but sometimes they'd wake up and he'd just have to get on with it. I was home at about quarter past eleven. It was only to help out, I got £4 10s. a week.

MAC: When she got that job at the cinema I used to sit at home on my own. Couldn't read, couldn't do nothing, and I'd sold the telly. During the day I used to help clean the house and mess about and then I was out looking for work. The radio went – Lily dropped her portable transistor and we only had the one that crackles all the time. So it was really nice here of an evening!

One time I did disapprove of Lily working. When she had no need to. I've been fortunate-like for the last three years and cleared a lot of debt. This is the point. If you want to live with a couple of old chairs and if we didn't buy furniture, well, I'd have three or four hundred pound in the bank. But you can't have it both ways.

I think her working it's a good idea, from the financial point of view and from the point of view that she's away from the kids during the day. It gives her a break. Living in a small place, it pulls you down being here all day with three young kids. By the time I come home at night she is worn out – her mind goes. The children cause real friction between us. There's argument.

LILY: We have 'Don't do that' disagreements. If Mac gets annoyed with the boy, like this evening, he got hold of him and dragged him into this room. I said, 'Don't do that, you'll only make him worse.' But the kids do go too far. They go the whole hog when they start. Kathleen is four and is a little madam and Jock is three. He completely ignores you if you ask him to stop doing something. He just acts deaf. And he screams and screams. The baby is seventeen months – he is a real monster! They were all lovely when they were little babies.

Our dog is like the children, out of control and cheeky with it.

MAC: As soon as they see the front door latch go, they start.

Screaming and screaming, just as I come in. There's nothing I can do about it. It's very embarrassing with the neighbours. It's something that you think won't happen and it happens.

LILY: The eldest one, Kathleen, went through a phase of waking up at eleven o'clock at night and she wouldn't settle down. She'd yell her head off for nothing. We used to have to bring her into bed with us. And Jock, he tried it on too. But he was easier. You could leave him to cry for a little while and he would go back to sleep. But the girl and the baby – they'd lie there and scream.

MAC: When they are out they are perfect angels. On the weekends I take them to the park to play, we don't go far but they are good, I'll give them that. But once they get home . . .

LILY: I give them a smack sometimes and it helps a bit. They go off and have a cry instead of throwing themselves about the place. When Jock's in that mood I really have to keep my eye glued to him. He throws himself back against the wall and he bangs the back of his head. He could really hurt himself like that.

I give them good food but whether they eat it or not is a different matter. They usually waste more than they eat, that's the annoying part about it. Jock and his milk – he usually knocks it flying all over the floor.

Sometimes I slam the door on the lot of them and walk round the block. But I come back. You can't leave the kids. They can't fend for themselves.

MAC: They started all this when they went to school, picked it up from the other kids. If one boy uses a new swear word, they all use it. If one child spits, they all want to have a go. But you've got to do the wrong thing before you know. You can't do everything right.

LILY: They like unscrewing the knobs on the drawers and pulling the wall-paper off. This hole in the chair, they done that. They kept stretching and aggravating it and now the cover's spoilt. I have to keep them in here because of the stairs, and the yard's no bigger than the bedroom.

There's no bathroom, but you can get a wash. It's very awkward with the kids running in and out if you want to get a good wash. If you shut the door they always rattle the handle. The toilet's outside and that's difficult with the little boy because he wants to use the toilet and won't use a pot. And if he wants to go out there I can't always rush downstairs straight away. He used to wet himself a lot but I find he has got quite a bit better since he has been at day nursery. They've got the toilets there and it's a novelty to him and he goes and uses them.

Now I've got this office job I get up at seven, or any time between then and half seven to give myself time so I don't have to run about too much. I get the kids up, if they are awake we let them come in but I try to get myself up and dressed first. Then I feed them, or they feed themselves, get them dressed then give them a quick wash. Then it's out, down to the nursery school and off to work. The youngest boy has a little cry when he goes in there. There is one woman he trails about after, he has taken a fancy to her. But they say he's ever so good during the day and they hardly know they have got him. They are very nice down there, very clean. I'm in such a hurry in the mornings I don't get no time to talk. I dash up there, 'Here are the kids, take 'em', and off I go to work.

MAC: I like the usual – having a few pints of beer. When I get a good wage we has steak every week. Not every day but at least once a week. I used to follow boxing, but I don't gamble now. I don't follow nothing else. Most times I'm at home of an evening. Saturday or Sunday is the only time I go in a pub like, other times I'll have a bottle in the house. It's the money like, now. I'm tied, I can't do much. If you haven't the money you can't do nothing, no matter what you want to do. I save for smokes, roughly one and sixpence a day, but it's more now I'm home.

LILY: We haven't been out together for ages. We don't go anywhere really. We asked my mother to baby-sit and it's too much trouble for her. And that was when we only had one baby, so we haven't bothered since. Sometimes the girl upstairs does but you don't like to ask anyone when you've got three little ones – if they do wake up they are little monkeys. My friend comes round sometimes but the last time I went to see a film was when I was expecting my first baby, about a month before he was born in April 1963.

As soon as the children are old enough they go out in the room of their own. I don't like them sleeping with us if I can help it. If they are ill we bring them into bed with us but if I can get them to settle back I'll leave them. It all depends on how tired I do feel. I think it is the only time we are together on our own and you might as well enjoy it while you can. I find that money troubles and all that, I mean, they don't worry me to *that* extent. I worry when I come to bed, I lie there thinking about money. But if my husband feels inclined . . . well, then, I forget about it. Worries don't come between us that much, not so as to disturb our sex life.

MAC: Children in the room don't affect me. It all depends on your virility. I'm highly sexed myself. I get too involved – you don't take much notice of the kids then.

LILY: We don't see my parents much. They live their own lives and we live ours. They honour us with a visit now and again. We borrowed a pound from them, but this has been paid back. You just never feel like asking them. They feel we shouldn't be short of money. It's a crime to them that their son-in-law should be like this. My general feeling of what Mum wants for me is something absolutely super. I suppose it's only natural to want the best for her daughter but she gets a bit beyond herself at times.

I had an argument with her once about it. She said she saw

my husband walking down the High Street one weekday morning. She said, 'What's he doing down there?' I said, 'He's going after a job' – he was in work at the time and had taken the day off to see about another job with better pay. 'Oh, he's always changing jobs', and she carried on. A couple of weeks afterwards my father came over and he said to me, 'I've come over for your mother to apologize', and I got a bit annoyed. Well, she should come over herself. But I've no hard feelings with them. It was an argument and that was it. When I told her that I had taken a full-time job and she come out with, 'Oh, good for you'. I could never imagine my mother doing what I do. Say it was a Thursday and I hadn't any money – I'd spent mine in the morning – and the light had gone out and my husband was coming home in the evening, well, I'd boil up a kettle on the coal fire. I could never imagine my mother doing that. She would have a fit and say 'Oh what am I going to do?'

MAC: My Dad used to have his own shop. He was a boot-maker and repairer. I left school at fourteen. My mother died when I was twelve and after she went, well, everything went. I looked after meself most of the time. We did have a general help but they weren't much cop. I went into the Navy and travelled all round. Came out before my time – just got fed up. I come out at twenty-two and lived all over, in Southampton, Portsmouth, Nottingham, Leicester, Bradford, all through the Midlands, Birmingham, Edinburgh, Inverness. I'm a painter and shop-fitter, belong to the Painters' and Decorators' Union. I was recommended by them to go in for a course to train as a branch official. If you're any good you get an average of £1,000 a year and a clean job with it. I used to read books, study and all that but I packed it in. Trade Unionism now is too much politics. It was supposed to be a non-political movement. I've done a big job at MGM Studios at Elstree, I was earning a clear £25 a week hanging paper. I've worked for Harrods, I could still be there but how can you stick at the same basic rate of 7s. 2d. an hour the minimum? I worked in a laundry but I wasn't getting sufficient money back. Also I had a dispute over fares, they weren't paying my fares from home to the job on an outside contract.

LILY: It was that and he had to do all the labouring too, unloading ladders and all that from the lorries. That wasn't his job.

MAC: I went to see the manager and said that there was supposed to be a strict Trade Union shop. At the time I was militant but I've calmed down a bit now. Then I had to clean the bins and arranged the bins and I felt it wasn't my job – it wasn't in the contract.

I don't like being tied if I can help it. If I was single again I'd join the Merchant Navy.

LILY: I've always lived in London, you can pin it down to Wandsworth, I've been strictly limited. I left a comprehensive school at sixteen, left before the end of the school year to do hairdressing. I did serve my time as a hairdresser – three years. But now I wish I'd stayed on at school and taken the course I was doing which was a commercial course. They did try to make me stay on, they said I had great promise with my shorthand and typing but I didn't want to know. Now I really wish I had stayed to do it.

I could learn to do shorthand again in the evening. This job where I am, there are very nice people there, very understanding, so with a bit of luck I hope to stay on there for a couple of years or more. I shall probably change my hours round when the boy goes to school. If my employer agrees to it, that's all right. If he doesn't he'll have to find someone else.

MAC: Since my parents' day, marriage has advanced, definitely. You could say I was stable now, more settled like with a wife and three kids. This is just one of those times. It will come back again.

LILY: I met Mac through a customer of mine at the hairdresser's where I worked after I left school. She used to come in and she was always going on about how wonderful her Scottish lodger was. I always imagined him six foot four with ginger hair and a big beard and a kilt. One day she said, 'Come back and have a cup of coffee.' So I did and that was when I was introduced to my husband all unsuspecting like! He saw me round to the station, took me for a drink, saw me on to the train, and then we met again a week later. Then we started courting regularly and that's when the trouble began!

Maggie Burton

The Situation. The conflicting interests of combining motherhood and a full-time job for the wife in a marriage where the husband has a declared interest against the idea. The couple have been married for over six years, and have two children under five.

The Wife. Maggie Burton, aged twenty-eight. She was educated at a secondary modern and technical school, and became a production assistant employed by a commercial television company. She is married to John Burton, scriptwriter and television playwright.

The Place. A detached house and garden in Berkhamsted.

MAGGIE: I became pregnant very quickly. It was really shattering because I gave up work. I don't think anyone thinks about marriage and you don't really know what happens until you get married. It's a bit of a shock and suddenly you are not independent any more. I don't have any financial resources of my own and this is a problem. It's silly because I don't go without money, but it is just not having my own money, and this is what gets me down.

After the babies I got depressed and sluggish. I used to get frightened of going to parties, and feel I had nothing to talk about. I was a bit nasty to the kids at times – I felt I wasn't getting enough out of life.

I was washing nappies on my birthday and I felt that on this day I should have a break from the nappy routine. I thought, 'I must get out.' Then the idea gradually formed of going back to my old job.

John was dead against the idea and we had appalling rows. He would say that he needed me and the children needed me at home. Then I would say that I didn't think I was doing anyone any good by being discontented, I would like to go back to prove that I could do it, and that this is all I need. I said just give me ten weeks away and I will come back a better person.

I used to argue that I wanted to go back to work, mainly to see if I could still do the job and hold an intelligent conversation with grown-up people. He would reply that he would feel it personally and that it was a slight against him as a husband and that he was lacking in providing something that I obviously wanted which I wasn't getting. This was the main thing – he felt he was being a bad husband.

He never mentioned money but I have a feeling that he probably thought that friends and people who mattered would think that I was having to go out to get some money. I don't think one ever erases that thought from any husband's mind, unless you have a real vocation like a doctor or teacher. He also thought I was going back to the world of television purely for the glamour of it and he didn't feel that it was a particularly worthwhile job. He thinks my work is superficial and there is a lot of sitting round drinking in the bar and chatting up the birds and he probably thought I'd be just another girl in the bar to be chatted up. He is very conscious of mothers being with their children, which I am too, but I felt I would be a better mother if I had a chance to go out and work again.

One day we had a row about the state of the windows in the house. I had refused to wash them, and that, I think, convinced him that I obviously hated it at home and I'd better go back to work.

So I did – I took a temporary job in my old field. Most of the time I shut the fact out of my mind that John was upset because I was determined I was going to carry this job through as far as I could. I really needed it more than he did.

I enjoyed doing the job, finishing it and putting it away in the filing cabinet and that was that, and remembering it as a completed thing. Housework and children go on from day to day, with the same thing over and over again and one never actually finishes. I also liked earning the money and I did like the idea of wearing good clothes all day long and having my hair done more regularly and having a good lunch on my own.

After six weeks of work I gave up – I had proved the point to myself. I was still capable of holding down my old job and the sulks at home made the strain too great. There was one other important reason – my husband had injured his hand badly and he needed me to drive him to work every day.

Apart from that I knew from the start that I couldn't keep the job on. The children missed me, I know Christopher didn't like me going. He used to say, 'Please don't go', in the mornings. But outwardly we didn't have any major problems. Had he started peeing on the floor or something then I would have stopped work immediately.

I couldn't have done the job without my then mother's help. She is now training to be a nanny. She was straight from school and needed the job as experience before she started. She was a friend of the family and the children had known her well for years.

When I worked I didn't really make much money out of it, although money was not the prime reason for doing the job. I just about broke even after paying the help at home, and covering the extra expenses concerned. I did buy myself some clothes which I really needed for the job, and I bought a new push-chair but that was about it.

It is now six months since I gave up full-time work, and the strange part is that I don't miss it at all. Yet my day at home remains seventy per cent chores. This morning, for example, I spent making lunch for John and the children – steak and kidney pie, carrots, potatoes and a home-made lemon meringue pie.

I don't believe in a set routine because at the moment the children are so young they need me to play with them a lot. My son will be five in September, so then I shall lose him completely to school. I try to devote as much time as I can to the children because I do love them. Our house now is always full of the neighbours' children and their pets – I think some of the kids feel they can relax at our place and put their feet up on the sofa. We are very doggy and animally ourselves – we have four cats and two dogs of our own. Also, I'm hatching a plot to rear chickens later in the year.

John wants us all to go away together on a holiday this year – renting a cottage in the country – but I don't really want to go. My garden is looking marvellous and I don't want to abandon my roses.

What still bugs me is having to ask my husband for money for myself. I feel as if I am always asking him, as I am, I am afraid. I think it is a very great responsibility for a man to be the sole provider. But I do earn a bit of pocket money as I've taken on a part-time job typing for a retired lawyer. I do the work after I have put the children to bed on the evenings when John is working.

Maybe I have conveniently brainwashed myself into accepting a situation that I am powerless to change. But that is only part of the situation. I am now in a much stronger position to make truer comparisons between the two types of lives – at work and at home. Really, John was right. My type of job is concerned with petty, unimportant, superficial details. Once you have done the job you have done it, and the routine becomes dull. I had built it up in my fantasy life bent endlessly over the soapy nappies. I had to get away in order to come back refreshed and able to go on.

But one remark made to me by my next-door neighbour I can't get out of my mind. She is a woman in her late forties who has devoted her entire life to bringing up her four children now leaving home. 'You must be careful,' she said, 'one day you may be like me with a cupboard full of home-made preserves and no one to eat them.'

Maureen

The Situation. A young couple are living in a dormitory suburb of a Midlands town. Problems of isolation and loneliness and lack of money govern the life of the wife, whose husband's job takes him away from home for long periods. The couple have been married for five years. There are two children, a boy of four, a girl of two and a new baby is expected soon.

The Wife. Maureen is in her middle twenties. She was educated at a secondary modern school, leaving at fifteen when she trained as a book-keeper. Her husband, Bert, thirty-one, is a linesman working on high pylons.

The Place. A two-bedroomed, semi-detached house on a big new housing development outside Bedford.

MAUREEN: I married when I was eighteen and Bert must have been twenty-two. I was square, backward almost. I lived with my parents and did everything that I was supposed to.

Bert used to come and knock for me and we used to go out. It was just how you read about or see in the films. Bert goes for anything like that, romantic and just right.

When we first married we saved for our house. I had always wanted a house of my own, a proper home. But we got rather selfish and first we bought a car, and then we changed that for a more expensive model. We could afford that when we were both working.

When the baby came along we took out a mortgage on a house on a new estate, but quite honestly, four years of life here is beginning to damage my marriage. It is like a desert, nothing to talk about outside the children and washing-up. We don't have many friends, Bedford people are hard to talk to.

Alone in the house I get very depressed, and with the children the same job crops up every day and after a bit it doesn't seem worth doing. Marriage becomes a job of bringing up children, not a partnership. We don't even share going out to the pub because one of us must always stay with the children.

There used to be a group of us mothers pushing our first babies to the clinic once a week but now that has stopped. It is too much effort to push two so far.

Occasional tea parties fill in the worst time of day from three until five when everything is done and we are waiting for the husbands to come back.

Without a car, and with young children, as I am, you are really stuck. Communication buses are so poor. I can't even get to the pictures in the evening on my own as the last bus back is at nine o'clock.

It's terribly quiet here, and not being able to drive I can't get about much to visit my friends. But I am booking up some more lessons and I'm really determined to pass my test, I am. I took driving lessons before but I could never imagine myself driving. It didn't enter my mind. I thought, 'I'm just taking driving lessons'. I didn't think I would really be able to drive on my own. I had completely the wrong attitude.

Sometimes I feel I'd love to go back to my job. I went back part-time when my eldest joined a play-group. It was just like a holiday. But now with the baby I've had to give that up. Sometimes I feel I'd love to do something with my evenings, but I never know what. I'd like to go to evening classes. I took French and I knew it quite well when I was at school. Now I've forgotten all of it because I haven't touched it since then.

We are not really planning to stay here but there is nowhere else to go that we can afford. I'm having another baby, and with three children you need quite a large house. I wish we had enough money, just enough not to worry about affording things.

I'd like a proper house, the usual, semi-detached, but with a garden and a wall and a garage. Our house is almost pre-fabricated, you can hear the springs creaking in the neighbour's bedroom adjoining ours, and the rows going on. I'll admit the central heating is marvellous. This house would make a nice oven.

There's no convenience. The kitchen, where I am usually, is too small, and it shrinks on the weekends when Bert wants to use it as a workshop.

I'm not houseproud but as soon as I've done the floor over, he comes in with his muddy feet and wants to bring the pieces of his car in. Naturally, I'm not keen.

But he has a go at me saying that you see adverts on the television showing men walking into women's kitchens and making a mess of them and that they have got these marvellous things that clean the floor with no trouble.

I want a garden of our own. The disadvantage of the open plan here is the problem of keeping young children on it, and off the road. I feel I have to keep them indoors with me all the time as I never feel secure when they go out on their own.

Bert works overtime and this bugs me because it means he has to go away for a few weeks at a stretch.

What is so awful about being without him is continually having children and women around. You talk different to them as you do to a man. You get to long to rush out into the road and have a sensible conversation with an adult, if you can still think of a sensible remark that is.

When he goes away, definitely the first week is the worst. I can't imagine what it is like to have a man in the house again, I can't imagine what it is like to wash shirts, to see shirts hanging around and picking up socks and his things.

When he comes back I get terribly excited, and there seems an awful lot to do. I can't cope with cooking a meal in the evening as well. Definitely the first two days are the worst.

When he's home I'm always thinking of going out with him in the evening, but I don't go, really. I don't think he likes taking me out all that much in company. I may suggest getting in a baby-sitter and he says, 'I don't want to leave the babies with her.' I think he feels more comfortable on his own. I'm ever so nervous when I do go out in company because I don't go often enough.

When he's away I don't go out on my own. I have been asked to the pictures by a man friend, but even though I knew he didn't mean anything by it, I wouldn't go. I'd feel terrible, and I wouldn't know what to say, on my own.

Living here is like living in a town but without the advantages of a town. The estate is two or three miles long from one end to the other, but it only consists of houses on one side of the road and on the other. Different parts spread on and on. This street, you could put it in a town and it wouldn't be out of place. If we were a bit farther out in the country we would be more isolated and it would be like living in a real village where everybody knows everybody else. But we are just near enough to Bedford to be a dormitory. Half the people here you have never seen or they leave before you get to know them. Being so near a big town it is neither one thing or the other.

Bert says that what we want is a community where you can mix in. There's no community spirit around here and people aren't involved.

There was a real crisis for me when Bert was away. My four-year-old, John, fell off a table and looked completely lifeless. I rushed to the estate telephone. My lucky day, it wasn't out of order. I phoned our doctor who lives on a nearby estate. He completely washed his hands of it and said I would have to take him to hospital. I knocked up our neighbours, and they weren't interested. So then I thought of our local midwife, who has a car, and she very kindly took us when I said I've got to get Johnny to hospital. At the hospital they kept him in all day and that night because he had concussion. It was the worst night of my life. I imagined all sorts of dreadful things and I cried all night. I had never left him alone before at night.

I did long for Bert very much. At times like that it is just awful. You have nobody to talk to.

Anne and Michael

The Situation. A time-table of physical separation combined within a framework of togetherness. Both the husband and the wife are engaged in full-time professional jobs. The couple share many of the domestic aspects of running the household and the care of their two children, aged two and three years. They have been married for seven years.

The Husband. Michael, in his early thirties. He is a violinist under contract to a nationally known orchestra working mostly in the evenings.

The Wife. Anne, aged thirty. She is a full-time university lecturer.

The Place. A small flat in a modern block in a London suburb.

MICHAEL: We didn't specifically choose our hours, but we had our chosen professions and the time-table goes with it. We chose each other and had to accept each other's work commitment.

By the time Anne gets back from college at about six o'clock in the evening I am ready to go to work. When she gets in we try to swop the most vital bits of gossip but this is a bit difficult with two young children who are also loudly demanding attention. This general chaos of non-communication lasts about twenty minutes and then I have to take over the car and buzz off to work. I'm back any time between eleven or eleven-thirty p.m. I usually have a snack in the canteen and I don't eat again. I certainly don't expect a meal waiting for me at home, but I do look forward to seeing Anne.

ANNE: I try to wake up at about eight o'clock a.m. and I am eventually cajoled or forced out of bed at half past eight. Michael gets up first and makes the tea and toast, so I just butter and marmalade my toast with the children's help, and eat it with the children's help. I leave the house by twenty past nine on a good morning and I drive to work which takes about fifteen minutes.

I always put the children to bed because this is the one time in the day during the week when I have any chance of seeing them. I have deliberately chosen that I should put them to bed instead of Nanny otherwise I would hardly see them during the week.

MICHAEL: On Sunday mornings I usually get the children up as this is Nanny's day off and Anne's one chance of a lie-in. I have a long sleep on one or two mornings a week so it seems only fair.

On Sunday last I came downstairs at eight o'clock because there had been a rumpus going on for about an hour. I gently admonished the children and demanded silence for the next half hour. I made myself a pot of tea and sat down with a book and a cigarette. They played quite quietly and chatted, in their cots, or they were supposed to be in their cots, but I made a point of not looking too closely. In twenty minutes they came in and they sat one on either side of me on the sofa and I told them a story. Then we set about getting up, which when Nanny is not here is an involved proceeding because I am not as highly organized as she. Nanny has a routine and the children just follow out of sheer habit. However, basically the job is simple. It is a question of removing nappies, washing bottoms and then persuading them to stand still in the right place whilst you supply them with clothes and put them on.

When they were smaller I was resigned to doing it but in fact I enjoy actively looking after the children now. They are more like reasonable human beings.

ANNE: I do feel tired most of the time but things are easing up a little. When the children were babies I was perpetually exhausted. I think I only kept going by trying not to think too hard about tomorrow.

I couldn't have attempted to keep my post without the help of a kindly and efficient nanny in whom we had complete confidence.

It wouldn't have been possible either if Michael hadn't taken over what really were my duties in the house. He did the shopping – in fact I don't think I went into a grocer's shop for about two years. And he has always been good about ministering to the children, changing their nappies, washing them and feeding them. When our first son was three months I took the decision to go back to work.

When the stresses of combining so much become almost unbearable, which they do periodically, I very seriously consider giving up my job. I feel I nearly give it up every six weeks.

MICHAEL: I'm inclined to be against the idea of her giving up. Anne has a job which, except when she is in a downcast state, she thoroughly enjoys and gets a lot out of it and it is a worthwhile job. I think that she might well find that to give it up and devote herself to being a housewife would be very limiting for her.

ANNE: I don't know. Sometimes I think that his enthusiasm for the morality of my staying at work is a rationalization of our need for more money. Although to be honest most of my money goes on employing people to do my job at home. But marginally, we are better off financially.

MICHAEL: I agree that money is the prime consideration but even if it wasn't I would want her to work, I am sure of it. I don't think it is necessary for children to have any one parent with them constantly for eight hours a day, provided that they have a stable home life. They see Mummy first thing in the morning, they see her at bedtime nearly every evening. Nanny is a constant factor except on her day off. I pop in at odd times during the day, I may see them for perhaps only half an hour at a time but I take Robert, for example, to my workshop and we do a bit of carpentry together, or if I have the morning off the children are always around. They usually say 'Can we come into the bathroom? Watch you get dressed?', and I usually say yes. So they come and scrub my back in the bath and then come with me into the bedroom and tear round while I am getting dressed. They get involved in the intricacies of electric shavers and tape-recorders and we potter about together.

ANNE: We don't run our marriage like this out of intellectual conviction. This is just the way life happened. But I do have doubts, obviously, about whether I am doing the best for my children by abandoning them all day to a nanny.

I think this is a decision which cannot be sorted out rationally. You have to experience the situation and see if it feels right. If you are able to balance the contending forces within you, maintain both your inner equilibrium and the poise of the external situation, you know you have got it taped – anyway for the minute. I am consoled in part by the notion that ultimately I will have more to offer my children and my husband by stretching my capacities at work than by staying at home. I do find it difficult to accept the idea of having to stay at home all the time without much paid help.

MICHAEL: We live much more extravagantly than we would or could if Anne did not work. The budget on my earnings alone certainly would not encompass much domestic aid at home for Anne – certainly no living-in help – and our food bills would have to be drastically cut. We tend to buy good quick grilling cuts of meat because Anne doesn't have the time to cook anything elaborate.

ANNE: I hardly ever have time to concoct a dish from left-overs which I would do of course if I was at home.

On Michael's money alone we would probably be able to afford a person to look after the children on one day a week, providing we didn't have to pay for an evening baby-sitter as well. At the moment I have a cleaner who comes in once a week but I think she would have to go if I didn't work.

I used to be a planner and a doer but now I merely think about plans and don't actually get round to doing them. Dreaded inertia sets in and nothing gets achieved beyond the normal routine. I think this is partly a by-product of a long-standing marriage in which we both try less hard, and partly due to my chronic tiredness. I aim to get to bed about half past ten. It would be much better in some ways if I could go to sleep and stay asleep when he comes in. I never get a long night's sleep and wake refreshed. But if I don't stay awake it means we miss our day's chat.

MICHAEL: Anne is very exhausted most of the time. I would be pleased for her sake if she could get to sleep early on but I would be very disappointed for myself.

ANNE: We do have Sunday afternoons together, plus the children because Sunday is Nanny's day off. We usually try to do something together with the children then, or friends come round. But we have learnt that if the children are present you can't divert your whole attention satisfactorily to each other or to guests.

MICHAEL: We have a long history of shared life dating back several years before marriage. We have known each other intimately for about nine years in all. We had a big affair before we got married although it was not directly followed up by marriage. We frequently kick ourselves for not having got married in the first place and then console ourselves by thinking, well, perhaps it was a good thing really.

ANNE: The great thing is that we have shared memories of idyllic moments. It is extremely important to us that our sex relationship has been intensely exciting in the past and some-how enriches what we have now. And if this experience had been with someone else and not with Michael, I might feel differently about the present. It is so marvellous that I married the man with whom I had this fantastically thrilling love affair.

When you are first in love and want to go to bed you say, blast whatever it is that duty demands should be done – the shopping, the cleaning, the ironing, the washing-up. But in marriage you learn that you can't leave the washing-up indefinitely. You have to take some heed of today in order to be able to live through tomorrow. By the time that the place has been restored to a liveable-in condition, your mind might be on the idea of making love but your body is through with it.

MICHAEL: One of the great disadvantages of my work, greater perhaps than the late hours I have to keep is that it absolutely drains me both in mind and body.

ANNE: Michael's work exhausts him in precisely that psychological area that is required to make love. He would probably be okay in the morning, but then I have to get up on time.

MICHAEL: We feel about sex as we do about money. We wish we had more of it but we enjoy what we have. We are completely intimate and honest with each other and on this basis admit that our sex life is not as exciting as it was.

ANNE: Michael saw both our children born and I am quite sure that this experience radically altered both our attitudes to the concept of physical shame. I wanted him to be there desperately because after all he was a partner in all this. During our love affair before we married we were as physically intimate as any two lovers can be, but I think that one would have preferred not to be involved when the other was going to the lavatory, for example. But after your husband has witnessed your having a baby, there isn't much left to surprise or shock him about a woman's physiology. So I don't feel any sense of shyness now about going to the lavatory when Michael's in the bathroom, nor he about going when I am present.

MICHAEL: We do share a bath, which some people I'm sure would find abhorrent, but this is largely for the prosaic reason that it takes twenty minutes for our bath to run and time is precious.

ANNE: On moods we react differently. It is usually possible to adjust our moods if one is feeling chirpy and the other is feeling not too bad. If we are both feeling tired and worn out then neither can give the other a boost. I drag him down more than he drags me down. Michael enjoys the moment much more than I do. I have my moments that I enjoy supremely but I don't enjoy day-to-day life in the way that Michael does and I think that his enjoying life as it happens here and now is perhaps linked with not wanting, not feeling, a need to plan ahead.

MICHAEL: I think the one thing that depresses Anne is the feeling of lack of plan, lack of objective, perhaps, of living from hand to mouth. I always have done so. I think it's a condition one gets into with my particular work. You are brought up to realize that it is a rather precarious profession even if you are, as I am, fortunate and have a regular job. This isn't a state of affairs which you can guarantee will continue.

I worry when I feel I am failing to do my work well enough. Then it is easy to take it out on my wife but I try not to.

ANNE: He goes rather quiet. Michael is rarely bloody-minded, really rarely. And I don't think he ever takes it out on the children.

I have sometimes felt that if only he would out and say it so that we could discuss it in the clear, we might get somewhere. But Michael keeps it all inside, and perhaps I will, and we don't actually recognize that each is worried about the same thing until some time later. In these situations we use as a protective defence a particular form of politeness towards each other. A bad omen. Neither of us can let off steam by having a blazing row.

There's a slight dichotomy in our attitudes, in that I would like to know that we had something invested, possibly in a house. So that if Michael had his hand chopped off and I were blinded, we would still have somewhere to live and a roof over our heads.

5. The Success drive

Kenneth and Elisabeth

The Situation. Feminine emancipation in practice within the context of long-standing marriage and parenthood. The wife is a successful careerist who holds a 'man's job' in a highly competitive profession. Her husband has built up a respected reputation of his own in a different sphere. The couple have been married for eighteen years and they have three children, two boys at boarding school and a baby daughter.

The Husband. Kenneth, in his mid-forties, a solicitor with a prosperous London practice.

The Wife. Elisabeth, in her late thirties. A careerist from the outset, she is a consultant physician who runs a department in two hospitals.

The Place. A large modern house and garden in a residential London suburb.

ELISABETH: I can't go back if I give up my post. I do the sort of job that is usually undertaken by a man – and I have a number of highly trained men working for me. In my profession I have applied for fairly high posts for which numbers of first-class men applicants have been rejected. Once I withdraw and resign I can't go back. In the eventuality of my finding life unbearably impoverished without my work I can't go crawling back to the authorities and say 'Look, I want another good job.' They will say 'Look how you have behaved, you undertook this, that and the other job and then you dropped it all like a hot brick.' This is only supposition. But I feel that at a subconscious level there is still a great deal of jealousy between the sexes. Women are not yet accepted naturally by men and our husbands as people who should go out to work.

If I could drop out for a year or so to see what it is like I would. But indeed now I feel I couldn't take the risk.

KENNETH: No she couldn't. It is for an entirely different reason. Whilst she is at work she is the equal of any man in her profession, the equivalent of anybody. Once off her own ground she might not find it so easy to justify herself.

ELISABETH: Don't forget that I am a failure at everything else. I cling to the one sphere where I am a success. With my two older children I somehow haven't made the grade. I haven't got much contact. I have always felt guilty about not spending enough time with the boys when they were small. I hardly ever saw them, but to be honest this was partly my temperament.

Right from an early age I didn't hit it off with my elder son and this was a great blow to me, perhaps because he is so like me. Largely because of this he was sent away to boarding school at the age of ten and he has always remained a stranger. As far as my second son is concerned I am closer to him. But again, all the time I wanted him to be perfect. You can't expect that of a child or of any human being, whereas with work perfection is a realizable ambition.

I think many of my problems are personality problems and not necessarily the consequence of my working.

KENNETH: She wanted children just like she wanted a car or a mink coat. And also to prove herself again, to show that as a woman she could be a mother.

ELISABETH: I wanted children. I don't know why. I wanted children very much. I couldn't imagine not having them. But again I am not sorted out. I can't explain why I feel the things I do. A psychologist would go back to basics. Why was I so intense about my work? Why wasn't I content to give up my job when I married and be content with cooking and ferrying the children to and fro? Reasons of one's background and upbringing come into it. Right from early childhood I remember my mother saying that I must stand on my own two feet – 'You must have a career, a profession.' Her own marriage was not a happy one. She felt resentful that she wasn't in a position to assist the family when my father's business failed. She had no job she could take because she had no training.

I had to prove that I could do it. In the early stages when the two eldest children were young I certainly put my work and my career first.

KENNETH: And where did she put me? In the dustbin.

ELISABETH: He has had to put up with a great deal. On the other hand, do let's be fair, an independently-minded person such as himself also likes to go his own way. Besides, why did he marry me in the first place? It was always a known factor that I intended to carry on with my job. He knew and he did.

KENNETH: I thought she was going to keep me, that's why I married her! Seriously, I didn't mind her working. I have never minded her working because I know she would be so dissatisfied without it.

ELISABETH: He is proud of me, I know that, but to some extent he resents my independence.

KENNETH: I understand the way she feels but I don't agree with her. I think you have got to opt in this world for one thing or another or compromise. My wife is psychopathically incapable of either consistency or compromise. Everything is black or white. There is no such condition as grey.

I know that almost every issue in this world is grey. To her everything must be clear-cut. If one asks a question, the answer must be yes or no. She can't qualify, her mind is incapable of accepting the need for qualification. To me, this is ridiculous in a person with her scientific training. I have never met anyone with such a highly qualified scientific training who in her approach to problems other than her work is so unscientific. There is no question of it, her voice on her subject deserves to be heard because she is a brilliant person.

She is right at the top of her field. But you can't bring that forceful dominating person at work back into the home because to bring that back seems to make a nonsense of what a home should be. All right, run the place like a university department or a boardroom by all means. But then don't, if the system breaks down, burst into tears and sob, 'Why do you leave everything to me? I can't be expected to bear the burden of it?' Nothing is left to her except what she insists on having under her control.

ELISABETH: There is an answer to it. When I work I am dispassionate. I am not emotionally involved. At home I am emotionally on the hook. As soon as emotions come into it I can't cope. Where it really matters to me, at home, I just don't tick.

KENNETH: She wants to be treated as a little flower at home and be petted and cosseted with remarks like, 'Did you have a nice day, dear?' and all that claptrap when she is feeling a fragile little thing. But, on the other hand, we are an Amazon. We are the equal of men, when it suits us.

A man likes to be master and to be petted but this is the reward, the service he expects in return for his role as the dominating partner. But a woman can't hope to maintain her place as the stronger party when every time it suits her she turns the switch and declares, 'No, no, I am only a fragile little blossom.' It makes nonsense.

ELISABETH: But I am the boss at work and everyone stands to attention. The whole place revolves around me and I am used to organizing. The power to control other people gives me a sense of satisfaction which perhaps I shouldn't enjoy as much as I do. But I know I am good at my job and that gives me the confidence I don't get at home because I am not a home-maker.

At home I like the place to be spotless and clean and precise but I can't create a homely atmosphere.

What he doesn't understand is that if anything goes wrong

at home – say the daily help doesn't turn up – I feel it more acutely than another woman might because my work is jeopardized. I have always taken pride in the fact that I never missed work because of domestic problems.

KENNETH: I missed my work instead. When there is a domestic crisis she leaves it to me to settle. I'm the one that is rung up. I cancel my appointments – we all know how trivial these are. But she carries on with her work.

ELISABETH: I'll tell you why. If you want women to be treated like men...

KENNETH: Who! me?

ELISABETH: If the country wants women to be given important jobs we must not have these handicaps and be dragged down by petty domestic considerations. But I have to admit I am lonely. I go my way, he goes his and there is a lot of friction between two such independent personalities. Apart from my work my one outlet is the baby. I feel very maternal towards her, quite unlike my attitude towards my first two. Now I have proved myself, I am not quite so intense about my work any more. I don't mind skipping the odd meeting if it gives me more time with my daughter. Nanny has every weekend off so then I can look after her myself.

KENNETH: One of my many objections is that the economic system under which we live means that the state gets the benefit of her valuable services, but that her net earnings do not cover the cost of Nanny. This is frustrating for her and I feel I am having to subsidize the state.

ELISABETH: I need a lot of domestic help to keep our house running smoothly. Our house has seven bedrooms, we are five in the family. I am out all day every weekday and my husband would not dream of doing the washing-up.

I have an au pair girl, a daily cleaner and a living-in Nanny. The au pair costs between £3 or £4 depending on how much work she does. The daily is £5 since S E T, and Nanny is about £8 10s. plus her keep. But wages keep on going up. I could not possibly afford to work and keep up reasonable standards in the house for which I need all these people around, if my husband was a poor man. I have the old-fashioned reliable-type Nanny – my job depends on her – who does just the baby, the baby's washing and who expects her dinner on a tray every evening.

On the nights when the au pair is off I get dinner, but after a day's work in the department I am pretty tired and I don't feel like peeling potatoes. Sometimes we do have a meal out in a restaurant but I feel guilty about spending the money. All these extra expenses come out of my husband's already heavily taxed income and I feel, and my husband does nothing to alleviate my conscience, that my working does not justify such extravagance. On weekends when the daily and the au pair are mostly off duty and the big children are at home, as they are during the school holidays, I never stop working.

KENNETH: The basic difficulty is that being a perfectionist she has to do everything as well in every other sphere, not only in medicine. No one person can hope to do everything perfectly. A man develops a sense of priorities and concentrates on those things which are important at the time. A woman, and Elisabeth in particular, doesn't seem to have this sense of priorities. In the morning, when she is in a hurry to get to her clinic, she will make herself half an hour late by arguing with our odd-job gardener about taking the Christmas tree out of the rockery, or she will have a row with the daily help about her running the washing-machine half empty – the load is below the maximum cubic capacity or some such consideration. Yet the cost of the electricity at stake is probably less than a penny.

ELISABETH: There is a right and a wrong way of running a home. Besides women are more obsessive by nature about such issues than men.

Sometimes I get to the point where I am a nervous wreck. Often I would give anything to be the next-door neighbour who is principally concerned with the happiness of the children and her husband, and who is fresh in the evening to go out. I have been out all day. All I want to do is to stay in.

KENNETH: But not to listen to me.

ELISABETH: I would like to chat but he always wants to sleep because he is tired.

Harry and Sarah

The Situation. A marriage between a former career-girl and a younger man. The husband's first encounter with his wife was in her role as one of the bosses at his office. She was the head of a department in the agency in which he was employed as a junior trainee. The couple have been married for four years and they have a six-month-old baby.

The Husband. Harry, aged twenty-eight, a Cambridge graduate who became a director of one of the leading London advertising agencies when he was twenty-five years old.

The Wife. Sarah, aged thirty-three. Shortly after her marriage she gave up her job.

The Place. A modern mews house in Hampstead.

HARRY: I was very taken with her when I first met her in the office. She is the kind of girl I always make passes at: self-willed, perceptive, aggressive, intelligent girls have always fascinated me and still do. I said to one of the directors, 'Does that girl screw?' 'I am sure she does if you would like to', he said. I found her very attractive, even though she is better looking now than she was then. She was in the rat race and trying not to be feminine. She had a wild temper and still has, she swore violently and swears violently. At the time she was breaking up an affair with a pompous middle-class ass called Rover after his car. She had been living with him for about a year and a half.

SARAH: I had virtually just left him at the altar – a very

dreary man. The banns were called and suddenly I couldn't face the prospect of life with such a boring person. So I was in a tough position, having 'independentized' myself.

HARRY: Sarah is five years older than me and when we met I was twenty-one and she was twenty-six. She was earning £2,000 a year which seemed an enormous sum to me having just come down from Cambridge, and she was determined to go further and do better. I was earning £700. She carried me completely in the first year at work and helped me much more than she remembers now or realizes. I got thrown in at the deep end and Sarah was someone who knew her job very, very well. She was exceptionally efficient. When I came to her with a problem or a situation which I didn't understand she would sort it out for me. If I had gone to anyone else with whom I wasn't having an affair they would probably have said, 'For Christ's sake take this away and don't bring it back until the job's done.'

SARAH: I emphatically never went through a sort of rapturous falling in love – whatever that may mean. An obsessed physical attraction is a quality I certainly don't feel for him. Initially, I was perfectly aware that he was trying to make me because he thought I might be useful to him – and why not? Ambition is a good enough reason.

We lived together in my flat for four years and then I objected to the principle of paying rent. Instead, I found a house, our present one, but I couldn't raise a mortgage on it. Harry became interested in the property and managed to get a mortgage through the Council and then there we were with a house on our hands. I refused to live with him in a house that my parents knew about so I wanted our relationship to become official. I suppose I sulked him into marrying me. I'm not a sulky person so when I do sulk it becomes rather noticeable. As if I was doing it on purpose.

Well, we were getting on very peacefully so why shake it all up? People don't like making traumatic changes in their private lives. I wasn't desperately anxious to get married. I was very happy in my career. It just seemed very futureless not being official; for instance no one in his department could know. So it was a question of marriage hinging on whether we signed the house deeds. It wasn't easy for him to up sticks and go. He might have had to leave his job which had enormous prospects. It would have been difficult for him if he had tried to get away.

HARRY: She didn't give me much choice. I was faced with the alternative of marrying her or packing it in. By that time I had become her boss at work – began as her junior and in four years was head of the department. I think she was in a very awkward position; after you have been living and working with a man for four years, it might not be so easy to find a new boy friend and a new job at the same time.

All these issues made our lives complicated and she became very upset and tense and cried a lot and even threw the sewing machine at me. Missed!

Part of the reason why I didn't marry her earlier was that she didn't fit the picture I had of the girl I would marry. I always said I would marry a pretty, rich, dark-haired girl and indeed I used to tell her that. I once told her so in bed and she burst into tears. I asked why she cried, as I thought I had made this clear all along. But finally, I decided to give in. Our affair was becoming an encumbrance at work and I always knew she would make a good wife.

I enjoy the masculine world and prefer to spend the evening with men, but I like to go home to a woman. My business engagements are just that – never girls with clients. I might play poker with the boys or meet one of my Cambridge or pre-Cambridge friends and start drinking at about 6.30 p.m. and end up eating with them. On the other hand I would much sooner that she came with me to formal parties or to dinner parties. I don't like going to parties on my own at all and if she can't or won't come with me I do get upset. I feel concerned if I'm out in the evenings more than two or three times a week, but as she chose to be at home all day I don't feel guilty about her being housebound.

SARAH: Harry is gregarious, and equable and dispassionate. He sees people's point of view. I'm ungregarious and very unfriendly. In a way, that is why marriage suits me because I have to meet only a few people when they are forced in upon me. Left to myself I wouldn't go out of my way to meet anybody. Before marriage I was forced into a type of market – you had to go to parties to look for a spouse as that was the thing to do. So marriage came as a great relief. I loathe going out to meet new people but I quite enjoy it when they come into my house, so I can meet them in my lair. Perhaps I want them to be at a disadvantage. Whatever the reason, it isn't anything to be proud of.

I do what Harry requires in the way of entertaining or being nice to clients, which isn't as bad as it sounds because I usually quite like them. It is really only in the last four months with the baby that I haven't been able to go out at all. The main reason is that we can't leave the baby with baby-sitters because she won't take her feeds properly from a bottle. On the evenings when we are at home together we do talk a lot. Harry is chatty – but not very revealing. Somehow now I have given up work and I am kept, I feel as if I am being paid to talk.

HARRY: When we first married we went out every evening and she never cooked. We would have drinks after work and go out to dinner in a restaurant because we were both earning quite a bit of money. She has become a good housekeeper now she has given up work, although I'm not particularly interested in her in that role. I am always telling her to do less. She could do other, more enjoyable things. I want her to have a nappy service. I want her to have a daily help. But she thinks these services are a waste of money and says she would feel guilty. It is true that our income has been reduced as she is not earning and we have the expense of a new house. We emphatically do have debts.

SARAH: I left work with the intention of breeding. I have had my career. I enjoyed it very much. I succeeded as much as I wanted to. I don't know what I wanted to prove – that I could make money, I suppose. I was earning £4,000 a year when I left. Now I am content for him to earn our money.

I am on my own a great deal and look after the baby. I work in the house all day. I cook a nice dinner for Harry on the evenings when he is home. Tonight I have a huge pile of ironing – very dreary. When he is late home I worry terribly that he has had a car accident and if it crosses my mind that he is with a girl I'm relieved. She's probably looking after him all right.

I've got this one thing, I have vague dreams about doing I don't quite know what, but something useful whilst I am breeding and being at home. I don't want to go back to my old job although I always can. When I was working it never crossed my mind to do anything else; the work was absolutely fascinating and I was passionately interested in it. But now I've got a slight reaction against. I feel advertising is immoral and I have an opposite urge of doing good. Perhaps my response is part of growing older. But I listen to Harry talking at dinner about the essential role of advertising in a capitalist society, very virtuously

I wanted to look after a foster-baby, to make a real job of it, but Harry wouldn't have one because he said it would disturb his nights. Beyond fostering I can't think of anything that I want to do which I would be good at. I shall think of the answer one day.

He does adore our baby. About the time of evening when he comes home she has a period of being irritable and he walks up and down stairs with her because this is the only treatment that shuts her up for a while. He walks up and down stairs with her in his arms until she falls asleep. I mean to produce at least one more baby and if he goes off with a redhead in the meantime – tough.

HARRY: I suppose there was a period when we were rapturously in love – about three days. By most people's standards I would say I still am 'in love' but I would not use the word myself, I haven't since my Cambridge days in fact. There are times certainly when I flirt with other girls, there are times when I would happily go to bed with another girl. We have been married three years now and I have no regrets. Sarah is less of a good mother than she is a good housewife. My relationship with her is extremely complex and I am glad it is. I get bored very easily with simple emotions. I'm not bored by Sarah. She still says things that surprise me, she irritates me, makes me happy. I still want her sexually, often. Seven years later, that seems quite a creditable record. There are very few of my men friends who haven't bored me in that length of time.

SARAH: Being married means I'm content. I have no grumbles apart from the fact that Harry only changes his socks once a week. We have a friend staying now and he has a small suitcase but the mess he manages to make with his few components is fantastic. It takes me an hour to tidy up after him. I realize how utterly virtuous and tidy Harry is. He might have brought his friend in just to show how good he is himself.

Sex isn't particularly important to me now, I think my present disinterest is related to having had a baby. I was fairly promiscuous before my marriage. Occasionally now I would like to be wantonly promiscuous. If I could do it utterly casually in the way a man picks up a tart it would be super. But I know it would make Harry so angry I daren't contemplate acting on the idea. I certainly don't dream of having an affair with someone – I can't think of anything more uncomfortable.

Ideally our marriage should be more passionate, but the

last thing I married for was passion. Not because the emotion fades but it makes life so damn complicated and colours everything with drama. I'm all for no-drama.

Emma and Jim

The Situation. A marriage between two unusually successful young designers who have formed a working partnership. The couple have been married for eight years and they have two children under five.

The Wife. Emma, an art-school graduate from a middle-class family, is in her late twenties. She specializes in textile design, interiors, and fashion illustration. She is expecting her third baby.

The Husband. Jim, in his early thirties, from a middle-class family background. He is an industrial designer.

The Place. A combined home and drawing office in a studio flat at Kew, London.

EMMA: After we first met, Jim kept in touch with me because he thought I had what he calls creative potential. After seven years of knowing each other he thought it was almost a duty to marry me, especially as I was clean and reliable too. He told me the other day that the reason he had wanted to marry me was that I was clean. What a reason to give – the girl takes a bath now and again!

JIM: I'm particularly concerned with cleanliness in appearance and habits.

At that time I didn't think I had the potential talent I considered that Emma possessed. I've changed my mind since those days, but then I thought she was a better bet than me in every way, both in terms of her ideas and her organizational capacities. I felt she could cope with being a housewife and taking domestic responsibilities as well as working. Also, she came from a professional background which I approved of – she had been taught to exploit her talents.

EMMA: I thought he was super and marvellous, the way girls do before they are married. In our partnership I have a lot of the ideas, I have endless enthusiasm and a ridiculous capacity for work, but he is a much better planner than I.

JIM: We work in a very specialized way, without having outside criticism and having to rely on each other's judgement. Emma is working on a project for me now which works very well so long as I direct it.

EMMA: I can't stand taking directions from him, I can't bear the way he gives orders. What happens when a wife works with her husband is that you think of yourself and feel he should consider you and make allowances for this or that personal consideration. I would never expect to find this sympathetic attitude in someone else who employed me, but I do from him.

I can't work if he is there watching me. I work in a completely different way from Jim. I have to let ideas just happen.

JIM: I expect her to understand the way my mind works and I know it is not easy for her. The trouble is that I'm so impatient – I'm that sort of person. I can't wait for her to make the usual great mess before she reaches a satisfactory conclusion which I know from experience she will do in the end. Her method of working is simply chaotic. To use an analogy, when I have to drive to some place I don't know, I will look at a map to see the quickest way of getting there. But Emma won't. She goes to Kensal Green by way of Beachy Head. I go through hell working with Emma, but I'm prepared to put up with her because at the end of it, I get better results from her than from anyone else.

EMMA: I have to be tremendously organized, as you have to be if you have young children at home, a home to run, and important work too. I have to plan my day very carefully, but I don't think Jim appreciates this. He comes in when I am working on my own project and tries to brief me on a job for him. I resent his assumption that I am free to do his work whenever it suits him.

JIM: She is a bad employee as she won't take direction.

In the early days I was working all day and every day, and when I came home at night I had no time for Emma or the family. Really, I had no choice. I sacrificed so many of my interests outside work – jazz clubs, classical music, reading, art galleries. It was a question of establishing a platform from which I could relax and possibly go away for a break. Also, I needed to acquire confidence.

But these days I am beginning to pick up the threads of my private interests again and I think I am much more sensitive and aware of the value of the arts as the result of my concentration on my design work. I see things in a more mature light.

You have to give up so much in the early stages of a career – but I was always lucky and my work went well from the very beginning.

EMMA: Never again will I undertake a full-time job with pregnancy. You feel sick, you feel miserable, and there you are pretending not to be pregnant.

We had a commission which created a commuting problem. We drove for two hours to get to the site every day, and there was me being driven through the snow with a bottle of Boots' indigestion mixture and being sick on the common. Meals out were a problem, I never knew where to go for lunch as everything smelt so sour.

The first month after I had my first baby the doctor gave me pep pills and calcium pills because I was so tired and unhappy and also I was finding my marriage a problem. The doctor talked to me and told me it was difficult to run a home, look after a baby and work too. Once I'd faced up to that fact I felt better. Just being told that I had a challenging job on hand helped me.

When I looked after our two children by myself I was totally exhausted, especially with the new baby and a toddler. One is

completely bound by the daily routine and I became a vegetable. It took an hour and a half to feed the baby sometimes
and I was in tears, he just wouldn't take it. There wasn't time
to read a newspaper even.

When the baby was a month old I went to an important
business luncheon. There were lots of people I knew there
and I felt an absolute frump. When they gossiped I wasn't in
on the conversation at all. For a month I had been utterly
devoted to those children and as a result I had nothing to
say.

Now I'm expecting another one, which I didn't want, and
there will only be eleven months between the baby and the
next one. I was desperate when I knew and felt like committing suicide. In fact I fixed up an abortion but my doctor
talked me out of it. Already I feel as if my brains have got left
behind somewhere, it's a horrible feeling.

JIM: I used to try and understand her reactions. She
explained that it was mostly due to hormonal imbalance. But
my own opinion was that the cause was due to lack of guts.
Cope with it, girl, I thought, cope with the situation.

EMMA: Bracing strictures don't really help, but I've learned
to live with his attitude. I put up with it and find my own
solutions. At least he is predictable.

After my first child I went wild and searched madly for
another man. I think it was partly because I felt the responsibility of the baby so very much and I resented the fact that
Jim appeared to abnegate all responsibility for the children.
Today I can see more clearly that in his own way, he did care,
but his general reaction was not to take any notice and I hated
him, I really did.

I found someone who was quite nice, but he wasn't really,
so that was all right.

JIM: I take the view that you can't base a marriage on sexual
loyalty. Probably many women and many men would like lots
of sex with lots of partners but it's so impractical. I for one

am too busy to upset my life for a mere fling. Besides, I don't find married sex at all boring. It can be perfect.

Perhaps I don't care very much about the importance of faithfulness. I think that honesty between us is all important – I know that sounds trite. If Emma undermined my attitude towards her by having an affair I didn't know about, that is what I would mind. The act of unfaithfulness, to me, is less significant than the deception involved.

EMMA: I expect Jim to be faithful to me. I feel our marriage wouldn't mean very much if I knew he was having affairs with other girls. If he did, I don't want to know. I know that is a very old-fashioned attitude.

JIM: I'm astonished she should expect me to be faithful. I find that explosively interesting! I'm the easiest man in the world to seduce, or I would be if I wasn't so busy.

EMMA: I accept his faults. If I can earn money and live my own life he will remain interested in me and not turn to someone else.

In spite of the expense we have a nanny now, and she is extremely good with the children and brings them up as I would and disciplines them as I would. We tried an au pair girl but she was an utter failure with the children, dirty, a nymphomaniac, and smoked a pipe.

JIM: Children just happen. I haven't a marked paternal instinct, and Emma hasn't any natural maternal instincts as such at all. The children are there, an extension of our lives.

EMMA: My mother belonged to the generation which devoted their lives to their children without a second thought. But you get to middle age and the children have grown up and gone away and there is an empty person who doesn't have any interests because there hasn't been any time. I would like my children to find me interesting when they get to the stage of needing a person instead of just somebody to put food into their mouths and change nappies. I am sure Johnny doesn't give a damn who changes his nappies.

JIM: Emma is hopeless with money. She just doesn't have any sense of responsibility about it, probably because there has never been a moment when she has not had money in her purse. The sort of thing I mean is that if there were two shops selling tights, and one sold them at 7s. 11d. and the other at 17s. 11d., she would go into the shop that was nearest even if the price was double the cost of the same thing in the other place. Also, she is so gullible! If she meets a girl whom she admires who says that Souflon socklets are best she will go out and spend hours looking for a shop that sells them.

EMMA: There was a time when we had a row about every dress that I bought. I used to keep new clothes in my cupboard for months before wearing them because I didn't want to risk a row.

I spend money as a kind of therapy. If I'm stuck on a work problem and I can't get anywhere with it, or I'm worried about a problem at home, I go out shopping and buy myself something. If I find what I really like it gives me a boost and I come back refreshed.

He thinks I'm extravagant, but fashion is a great influence in my life – as it must be. It is very important for me to be well dressed from the point of view of my work.

We don't have any real money worries now, but when we were first married we had very heavy commitments. I had my babies privately, not on the National Health, and he used to come into my room at Queen Charlotte's with a boot face thinking, my God, this is costing us a fortune.

JIM: I don't spend much money on myself because I don't need to. We don't spend all we earn because we are saving for a beautiful house which will be filled with beautiful things. Things matter to me enormously, and I have developed very expensive tastes.

Joan and Michael Bakewell

The Situation. Both husband and wife work in separate branches of the communications business. Unlike the husband, the wife is widely known to the general public and earns the larger salary of the two. The couple have been married for eleven years and they have a daughter of seven and a boy of four.

The Husband. Michael Bakewell, aged thirty-six, a Cambridge graduate who relinquished the administrative post of Head of Plays at the BBC in order to concentrate on the creative job of directing plays.

The Wife. Joan Bakewell, aged thirty-four, a Cambridge graduate. She has established herself as one of the all too few pretty women who have succeeded as an interviewer on intelligent television.

The Place. The Bakewells' house in Camden Town.

MICHAEL: Joan does enjoy her work very much. On the one hand I think, this is great, this is marvellous. Occasionally however, and it happens when I am tired, I lapse into instinctive ways of thinking – 'Hello, hello, the dinner is not quite what it ought to be, why hasn't all the shopping been done?' It's habit. Men have been trained for generations to expect these services of women.

But I don't want a homely little wife with the slippers put out beside the fire. I would hate it.

JOAN: To me, my life is not divided. It's all me. I never think of myself as a wife as being separate from the rest of me. It's all me, and I happen to be married.

I don't let the housework get me down. I am perfectly prepared to live in moderate squalor from time to time and then have a good tidy up. The suburbs are full of housewives settled with children after having a secretarial career and who thought it would be wonderful having two cars, clubs and coffee mornings. But there is a great neurosis among women who find that this life is not enough and the fun is over.

The whole feeling that a woman's role is concentration on embroidering cushion covers, flower arrangements and nappy rash, is all wrong. Sure, I worry about nappy rash but I solve it and get on to something else. Being a good wife is being an interesting person.

MICHAEL: We began by her being interested in my world of actors, writers and fellow-directors. She was happy, but there was always this feeling that she wasn't taking part in it in her own right. She was being simply my wife instead of being herself absolutely full tilt which she now is. This was basically the problem of the under-employed graduate wife and her frustrations which created a feeling of guilt in the over-employed graduate husband.

JOAN: When I had my first baby I expected to give up work. I thought I would be so overwhelmed by a child that I would want to be a mother and cease to be interested in the nonsense of life. But when my daughter became a little older I became restless. I like to be pushed to the limits, I like to know I'm taxing all my energies. Unless I have a deadline to work to and subjects I have been told I must think about, my mind gets lazy.

I am tremendously lucky to be doing a job that I enjoy. I do three or four programmes a week. On those days I go to a morning meeting from twelve until one; I am available to do recordings during the afternoons although our programme aims to go out live at eleven at night. On my programme days, I go to the studios in the evening and return home at about one-thirty a.m.

My working day routine is to take my seven-year-old daughter to school in the mornings and ferry my son to his play-group. If I need to, I dash to the hairdresser's. I don't go on great shopping expeditions these days because I have got my eye in and I know what I'm looking for. I can make a sortie to the West End in three quarters of an hour, park the car, dash into a shop, flick through the rails and home.

Then I ferry my son back home and the mother's help gets lunch. I dash to my meeting at the studio and come back to collect my daughter from school and I'm at home for their tea. I usually bath them and put them to bed unless I'm really pushed and then the mother's help does. I just keep going working through Christmas, the holidays, elections and weekends. I work on alternate weekends.

I don't think Harriet minds my working or not being at home all the time. She expects it in a way. This is how life is, we all go off and do things – she goes off to her ballet class. I can't recall a 'Why-isn't-Mummy-here?' crisis when the children really needed me to be there and I haven't been. I am at home a lot of the time.

I don't think I could manage without the car. I drive everywhere. Michael does not drive and he goes on his bicycle. When people hear that I can almost hear the sharp intake of breath. 'Ah,' I hear them thinking out loud, 'so SHE has the car? I wonder how those two really get on?' So I enjoy playing it up a bit.

MICHAEL: It is all part of my martyr complex.

On the child question, it isn't necessarily a bad thing for children to grow up without this slightly cloying, slightly claustrophobic closeness with their parents. Kids tend to get what they need out of a home anyway, and I find they adjust much more readily than one would expect them to. They feel that Mum is the focus of the home even though her time is limited.

I grew up in a very close family and as a result I think I developed as a person rather late. My children are encouraged to get to know many more people a lot earlier and they will be able to stand on their own feet earlier.

Joan's work is mostly in the evenings. The children see her during essential spells during the day and they don't seem to be suffering a grievous sense of loss because her presence isn't constantly at home. The fact that if they wake up at ten o'clock at night they find me or a mother's help hasn't proved catastrophic. If anyone is lacking half the time it is me because I am not there during this vital bedtime stage.

Going through the period of having a new foreign girl to help is always a slight upheaval for the children and for us. They arrive not knowing the house and not speaking English.

At first, when we were living in a much smaller place, we could never talk to one another properly because there was always a third person hovering about. But we have got used to that rapidly. We now have a system of giving her a place of her own at the top of the house.

JOAN: The men I work with are understanding but they do expect me to work as anyone else works. I don't claim any privileges so there is no particular feeling that children are a liability in my job. But it is known that I must lead a more highly organized life than the others. They know I like to work at home more so I can be with the children during the day.

I find it hard to unwind after a programme when I get home, and I can't go to sleep immediately. I do get tired but I have a lot of nervous energy and I catch up somewhere.

MICHAEL: Having a life that is by its own nature packed with people, I don't have a feeling of loneliness when I am on my own at home. Work naturally expands to fill the time available. There are always people to see, scripts to read, films and plays to see. Certainly there is not so much enjoyment in doing it by oneself.

My work has always continued on into the evenings, and at one time Joan used to sit around at home waiting for me to come in, so now a certain amount of frustration on her part has been relieved.

If I worked set and regular hours and did not lead such a hysterical life myself, and came back every evening at the same hour to a lonely little homestead, I can see that all the various resentments would creep in.

JOAN: I am not sure what he does when I'm not around at home. He probably works or makes notes or goes to see an obscure film – he enjoys that. He will probably do without food. The most I could hope for would be for him to open a tin of soup. He watches my programme and will answer the questions I ask him afterwards. But he doesn't volunteer too much.

He is in bed and asleep when I get back from the studios. He will try and say what he thought about the programme and there will be a few murmured exchanges, but we don't really communicate until the following morning. We meet at breakfast but we don't have too much to say at breakfast.

We are not away from each other in any sustained sense at all. We are on the telephone to each other a lot of the time. We know exactly what each other is doing so we don't feel separate even though there are periods when we don't meet.

MICHAEL: The disastrous weeks are those when we get out of phase and I'm free when she is working, and she is free when I am working. This is chaos.

We are now going to come to one another with more fixed points each during the week. My job has changed and instead of fixing my life round her, letting the evenings when she is free guide the evenings on which I work, I shall be less flexible and this is going to be a new problem to solve. If we are able to plan our lives sufficiently far in advance so we can coordinate our free time it will be all right.

JOAN: During the times when Michael has been able to stay at home it is absolutely gorgeous to sit around and have cups of tea and talk.

We try to organize isolated mini-holidays together of about four days off. You can make a lot of four days together. When we are in a gulf of not seeing each other and flying in and out of the house we know there will come a time when we will have a real break and get away together.

At the end of a long spell of work one of us will take the other out to dinner – it is like the early days of going out. We don't see many other people because we cherish so much the time we have together and our social life does suffer.

I now have a rota system whereby I am told a month in advance what nights I am wanted, so that I can plan ahead and have more social life. I do have the right to say 'I'm going out to dinner.'

MICHAEL: When we go away for a long weekend life clicks naturally back into position again. It is a matter of being determined to keep some weekends free for each other as we might both be working on Saturday and Sunday. But when we do get away the time is very valuable and good.

I travel quite a bit on my own which is a problem for Joan because she is on her own then with the family. I go away to see places or to attend conferences which I enjoy. I like travel for the sake of it – the moment you get on a train you become a different person.

We went through a phase when every time I went abroad some disaster occurred at home. Once, Joan tripped upstairs carrying a pan of boiling water which splashed over her face. For days afterwards she had to be televised showing the back of her head only. It is amazing what you can do if you are determined.

She keeps going. There was a bit of a problem with our second baby which she wanted very much at the time. She was on the brink of building up a reputation as an interviewer and it did mean taking off quite a bit of time. But she just managed to get it in without staying away for a damaging length of time.

JOAN: When I was doing work in which I wasn't interested I used to live for our annual holiday. But it never occurs to me now to think about holidays more than a fortnight ahead. It is lovely when it happens and we generally take the children with us, but my life isn't geared to wait for holidays. To have to struggle through the year just for that two weeks on the Costa Brava is simply heart-breaking.

MICHAEL: I lecture quite a bit and I am beginning to find that people tend to be more interested in what my wife is doing than in my job, and this is a new angle. But I haven't met this situation of generally being introduced as her husband – though it has happened perhaps two or three times. But I can see that the way things are building up this might become a bit of a bother.

Joan earns rather more than I do at present, but I don't feel any kind of rivalry. On the contrary I find it rather comforting. Perhaps I am consoled by the fact that Joan is freelance, her money depends on how hard she works, whereas I am staff and I can work round the clock but my salary is fixed to a rigid scale. I find this marginally depressing as far as I am concerned, but however much money we earn we always seem to be broke.

There are times when she gets tired and wants a simpler life. She certainly woke up feeling that way this morning.

Any job which begins at eleven o'clock at night is tiring, particularly any job which involves a considerable amount of preliminary swotting up. She described it the other day as a perpetual crash examination course in which you swot up a subject all day then you are tested on it in the evening, and the following day you have to tackle a fresh theme. Mercifully, most of her subjects are the ones we can talk about because her work does tend to fill her mind a great deal of the day.

In our life, the situation is constantly fluid, calling for perpetual readjustments. If, for example, she was to move into a completely different area, working in a different atmosphere, with different people in a different place, then we would be in two totally different worlds and this could conceivably constitute a problem. But thinking of the number of hurdles which we have cleared I don't see even this one as being insuperable.

In our relationship, you mustn't hold too many prior assumptions about what marriage should be.

JOAN: I wish there were more hours in the day to do all the things that need doing because I enjoy them all. I wouldn't give any of them up. But I think it is a splendid way to be, to have so much to do that you can't fit it all in.

6. *The class image*

Linda and Chris Parsons

The Situation. A working-class teenage marriage precipitated by pregnancy. The couple married when the boy was eighteen years old and the girl was barely seventeen. They have a baby daughter of eighteen months.

The Husband. Christopher Parsons, aged nineteen. He left school at fifteen and is employed as a skilled machine operative.

The Wife. Linda Parsons, aged eighteen. She comes from a large, united family. She left school at fifteen after taking a shorthand-typing course.

The Place. The couple's bedsitting room in his mother's council house at Chadwell Heath, Essex.

CHRIS: Lin wasn't blonde when I knew her first. She was carrot colour. Most girls, young girls, are skinny. But she wasn't, she was plump. I wasn't really mad on girls. I didn't mind going out with them but I wasn't terribly mad on I must have a girl friend. It was just that I knew Linda. It was easier than going up to a girl you don't know and asking her to go out.

LINDA: Chris was one of the crowd, and the crowd used to go out everywhere. At the time, I was going round with a boy who was his cousin. Then it started. We became a foursome, a girl friend of mine and Chris's friend, and then it ended up as two. We kept talking about getting married and joking around. Then it happened so quickly I can hardly remember that far back.

CHRIS: When Lin and I were going together I went out with another girl, but Linda didn't know. But everything I said to her was wrong. I only went out with her for a night but she used to turn round and say, 'Oh, that's not right', and things like that.

LINDA: When I told Chris I was having a baby he didn't believe me. 'Oh no', he said, and I said we can't get married because he wasn't earning a lot. I wouldn't have got rid of her because I know somebody who did try and the baby was born crippled so I told Chris I'd never try anything.

CHRIS: I wanted the baby. You like to know she's yours and you're going to do your best for her and bring her up as you want to bring her up because she is part of you and your life. We would have waited longer before getting married but I think I would have married her in any case.

I told my Mum the situation and she said, 'It's up to you, whatever you do it's your decision, your life.' She says she's not worried, 'If you want to marry her you marry her. But if you don't,' she says, 'it won't worry me.' But she said that she'd rather I did. Mum liked Linda, and so did me cousin and me Aunty liked her a lot. They were pleased in the long run.

We got married on the Saturday and I stopped work on the Friday. I didn't have a job the next week. But it was all right because Lin was earning. Linda's Dad, he gave us a nice reception and paid out a lot for it.

We live around me Mum's. We've got our own bedroom, it's not very big but it's our own and we don't pay no rent. We give Mum £4 a week for the two of us and the baby and she cooks all our meals for us which is very good.

LINDA: We give her the money and we have to have what's there, or go without. My mother-in-law does all the cooking and the shopping. I get up early, about seven o'clock. Then I lights a fag and get the baby up and wash her and dress her and give her her breakfast. Then my mother-in-law takes her out. I get our bedroom cleaned out – we're not allowed in anyone else's bedroom. Then I do my washing and the sheets and that in the sink and a bit of ironing I have to do and that's it. I don't eat nothing all day, not till we have our tea. Sometimes the baby has a bit of bread and honey at dinner time and that's all until her tea.

I don't get on marvellously well with Chris's Mum. We have arguments about the baby mostly. If she's got the baby and I say, 'I'll hold her now,' she says, 'No, you can't have her.' Once she's with them, they won't let her go.

CHRIS: I usually take Linda's side. She is me wife and I ought mainly to take her side. But sometimes she is wrong and then I tell her.

My Mum took the baby out one night. They went to see the lights in London and they didn't get home until about half past ten and they said they were going to be home at eight. Linda was going to have a row as soon as they come in. We didn't know what happened. It could have been crowded trains, or they could have got on the wrong train or anything. She wasn't going to ask. She was going to have a row. We ended up having a row about her not finding out what happened first. Then it settled down. She didn't ask what happened, me Mum didn't say what happened, and after that, nothing come of it.

LINDA: She got a terrible cold from coming back late.

I won't give in first in an argument. One morning he says he wants a clean shirt, and he doesn't look. I sit there all cool like and I say, well, I'll wash some tomorrow, knowing that there's a clean one ready right under his nose. I see how far I can go, tease him a bit.

CHRIS: I got up in the morning and done me nut because I couldn't find a clean shirt and I didn't think that Linda done any washing. She didn't say nothing, just layed there in bed, and I was hunting all over the bedroom. Then I found one. I knew I was wrong so I said I was sorry that that was it and we were back to normal.

LINDA: I'd go without a lot, almost everything, to get a place of my own. Then the baby could do what she likes. At his Mum's she can't really crawl around and do anything she

likes. Sometimes we have to sort of get her out of the way.
I'll be able to do my own cooking – I love cooking. I'll be
able to do me own shopping. I'll ask me friends in. And I'll be
able to come down me Mum's more.

We are on the list for a council house but Chris's Mum told
me once that we'd have to turn it down because he doesn't
earn enough. But I believe I could just scrape through.

CHRIS: We'd be running tight. With my present wage and
tax stopped and everything I get about £12 clear easy. If we
have a house you've got £5 10s. for the rent and the electricity
included, £2 for the Club, that leaves £4. We don't eat a lot
at home, like we've been living round at Linda's Mum for the
last two weeks.

We've got a lot of Christmas Clubs, it's a loan club at the
local pub. I've got one, Linda's got one, and we've got one
for the baby. I pay five shillings a week, Linda pays ten
shillings a week and the baby pays two shillings. It's sixpence
a share, so for me five shillings, every six months I draw ten
pound out. We have to pay it back over twenty weeks.

If we moved now we'd have to do without little luxuries
but I think we could just about do it.

LINDA: He's good that way – he doesn't milk his pay
packet before handing it over. And we've got about a hundred
pound coming Christmas that's been paid in.

I'd like to go out to work, even just a part-time job book-
keeping and typing to earn a bit of money and save. I'll try
and get one, temporary for a couple of months, I can pick up
about £10 a week mornings only if I go to London, or locally,
the wage for the same time is about £6.

My mother-in-law would look after Michelle. If I have to
start early in the morning I won't get the baby up. I'll just
leave her in bed and when she wakes Chris's Mum will dress
her. When I come home she'll be all ready for me to take
straight out and for the rest of the night I'll stay in and look
after her.

If we get a council house and I go to work I could leave her at a clinic. You pays them so much an hour and they look after the baby as long as you like. If not, I'll take her up to me mother-in-law's and she'll look after her.

I wouldn't really like to leave the baby in a clinic. I think there's so many babies in there you're not sure whether they are looking after them properly. I'd hate anything to happen to her. I wouldn't leave her for long because she frets. Say from nine until one o'clock longest. Really, I'd rather have me mother-in-law, with only the one baby to keep an eye on, look after her.

CHRIS: I'm not struck on the idea of leaving Michelle in a clinic. When I'm occupied at work now I don't think about her a lot – I know she's all right. But if she was in a clinic I would be inclined to think about her a bit more, is she all right and this and that and what's she doing? I'm not keen. But it's very important for us to save. It doesn't matter how much Lin earns. If she's only bringing home three pounds a week clear it helps.

As soon as I earn a good wage, say £18 to £20 a week, I'd like her to stop at home. She only works for the money. I don't think she fancies going out to work, she'd much rather be in the house. But we haven't lived on our own and I've no idea of how the money goes.

LINDA: Being married has its good points and I'd rather stay home with the baby and that.

We don't go out a lot. We used to go out in the evenings together when we first married, with the crowd. But most of his mates have got girl friends now. If he goes out with them it means they've got to get in a girl for him and of course he doesn't feel very safe.

In the last six months we have been to the pictures a couple of times and we went to a club with friends at Christmas, otherwise we go out with the family.

In the winter he comes in so late from work we don't have

time to go anywhere. Sometimes he stands and watches other girls, but he doesn't have a lot of time, really, for other girls. Sometimes he comments, she's marvellous and that. But I couldn't imagine us breaking up.

CHRIS: I think we will go through life together. I tell her I love her lots of times, just naturally, like when I've had a hard day at work or when I've got the hump and we have an argument, I tell her afterwards. When we are going out somewhere and she dresses up nice I might say she's my little darling. But I'm not possessive, not really because most of my mates are engaged anyway.

LINDA: He loves me, I know that. But you take it for granted after a while. If I'm sitting around and if he hasn't said it for a while I think, 'I hope he's all right', but I don't sit worrying.

Sometimes he'll come in when me hair has been rolled up. He'll say it looks nice but he says it in such a way that it didn't look nice last night!

Before we got married he used to buy me dresses and chocolates. If I went out and saw a dress he used to say, 'I'll buy it for you.' He still does but not so often. I get a bit worried at times and say, 'Have you got the money?' Last week he bought me some shoes and a skirt and some jumpers.

In general I make do with what I've got. Being married you don't have to keep up with the fashions. It doesn't matter so much because you don't go to dances and that.

CHRIS: Lin don't get much and every bit helps. So I buy her presents, not for any special reason, it just makes a change. She says she likes something and if it's not too dear and I like it she always gets it near enough.

LINDA: Seventeen is a nice age to get married because the babies can grow up when you are still young. It's better than being fifty when your children are young because you get a bit tireder then.

CHRIS: When you marry you become wiser with your

money. All my mates, all they can do is go down the pub every night and I don't see no enjoyment in that. We've got something we want to save for and we save for it. When you've got it, you've got the joy and satisfaction that you saved for it and worked for it. We've saved and bought quite a lot of furniture and I'm really pleased about that.

We don't nag each other and we've got near enough the same interests. I like doing models and she likes doing them. We buy plastic models in the shops and we stick them together and paint them. She always wants to have a go and she can't do them, she never can. But I think that keeps her wanting to have a go more and more. We have a little bet now and again, not every week but when we've got a bit of spare money we have a flutter. Lin's worse than I am sometimes.

I did like Bingo but it's got boring. Linda still goes but I don't like sitting there all night and marking off the numbers. In the evenings we talk about what we are going to do with the house when we get a house and how we are going to furnish it and what's going to happen to the baby when she goes to school.

When we bought a dining-room suite Lin said, 'You must come and see, it's really nice.' I went down, had a look and said yes, and it was ours.

We have our disagreements about the house. She wants a gas stove and I want electric. She reckons gas cooks faster and its not so dangerous – like leaving a hot plate on and then leaning on it. But I reckon I like the electric one – also in a council house the electricity is included in the rent. I expect she'll win, she always does so she most probably will this time as well. Not that she's the boss. Mucking about she might push me on the shoulder and say, 'Don't do that', but I know she don't mean it, and I still go and do it. No one's the boss, we give and take with each other.

LINDA: If you enjoy babies you don't think about the work involved. She does wear me out a bit, and I've only the one, but I don't care how many I have. Well, I'd like to keep it down to four. I'm happy if I've got babies round me, not that I have them that easily.

Michelle was three weeks early and I was thirty-eight hours in labour, but I didn't mind. It was rotten at the time but they give me the baby as soon as I'd had her and you forget. I was so excited having the baby to hold that I thought it was quite easy. Me Mum and Dad had an afterthought baby two years ago, so now Michelle's aunt goes in the playpen with her. I think seeing Mum's new one sort of brought it out in me.

CHRIS: Spaced out over the years I'd like three or four. I don't use contraceptives now and Lin doesn't take the pill. I never really believed in them. If you're going to have a baby, have a baby.

LINDA: No, I don't believe in it a bit.

CHRIS: I would have been a father at sixteen if I could have, I wouldn't have worried. I love little babies. I liked my little cousin. When he was small I was always up there playing with him and his motors. I was going to work then, everyone thought I was a nut. I never had a baby round me in the family because I had a little brother but he died.

Soon as I get home I start to play with Michelle. I have me tea and then little periods during the evening she runs to me and she gets a bit fed up. She goes to Lin, and she gets a bit fed up. Then she goes to someone else then she comes back and goes round again.

When she was a small baby I changed her nappies, I dressed her and bathed her. Now I can put her to bed, put her on her little pot, give her her drink and food, but I don't do it every night. Just when I feel like it.

LINDA: The baby sleeps in the bed with us. We have got a cot and she does sometimes go in there but at the moment it is full of wedding presents as we've got nowhere else to put them.

CHRIS: We can keep an eye on her. If anything happens you

know she is there and you don't worry so much. You can get to sleep quicker knowing that she is in the room with you. We usually put her in the cot if we want to have each other but when she's older I don't think she'll sleep through.

LINDA: When Chris wants to . . . well, we put her in the cot for that. But if she wakes up and cries we bring her in with us afterwards and she goes in between us.

I'm usually half out of bed anyway. I prefer it like that because if she is on my end I'm frightened she'll fall out, and if she's on his end usually the covers come off.

CHRIS: When we get up in the morning I throw her on top of the bedclothes. I tickle her tum and I hide under the blankets and pull them back and go 'Bo' and she sits there and laughs. Then she goes for walks over your head and punches you but it don't matter. You can't smack her because it's you got her into the habit of playing with you. I like her little bum and her hands, especially her little thumb and her little finger.

One day she was sitting there and she was playing with me eyelashes but she got her finger and thumb and poked them in me eye and she wouldn't let go. I had to smack her in the end because it was hurting. She's never done it since, she knew that she was wrong. She still smacks me in the face, but she doesn't go near me eyes at all. Michelle likes to be near someone, she likes to feel somebody near her. She's always pushing on me all through the night and I'm right up against the wall and she's right near me.

In bed I've got me arms round her and she's close. Sometimes I hold her hand with me other hand and she's off in about ten or fifteen minutes. I've got the other arm right over me, the baby and Linda so that I can cuddle all three of us. Then you're all in bed together and you know it's your family.

Patricia

The Situation. A young wife has reached the end of a whole phase in her emotional life. She has fallen in love, married and produced a baby. At this stage, she is able to assess the oscillations of her emotional seismograph.

The Wife. Patricia, in her early twenties, from an upper-class family background. She is an arts graduate, and has been married for three years to Robert, an Anglicized Czech. He is in his mid-thirties, and is an executive in a firm of management consultants. The couple have a daughter of two and a half.

The Place. A small flat in Highgate.

PATRICIA: From the moment I got engaged I felt completely disillusioned, resigned. Oh well, this is it, might as well get married. And I moved out of a whole phase of my life which had been operating since adolescence, thinking of who I would marry. Peeling apples and seeing what letter the peel would come out to and that would be the first letter of his name. Now you peel apples and throw it over your shoulder and find it doesn't make any difference – you are already married to an R.

I was in love, so I got married. I felt very matter of fact, not a bit starry-eyed or up in the air like in women's mags. The test was could I do without his presence and his company? I couldn't. We saw each other all the time every day and as much as we could before we got married. He had to go to Basle for a week and I said, 'Goodbye, see you next week', but after two days it was shattering. He had gone and I couldn't bear it, it was a terrifying feeling. Then I still wasn't sure, and I used to have these awful conversations with Mummy about whether I really loved him or not. I think she always wanted me to marry an Englishman and an aristocrat.

Our honeymoon was catastrophic, I think most honeymoons are. We spent two sumptuous nights at the Ritz which cost us over £100 when neither of us felt at all well. The next day he came down with raging tonsillitis and I spent our third honeymoon night feeding him oranges while he tossed and turned with a temperature of 102.6. He was almost in a state of delirium but he had preserved his sanity to the extent of moving to a cheaper hotel in the country.

His mother and her family get on my nerves. We have to visit them and it is sheer agony for me from end to end. Physically they just give me the creeps. It's not their fault – they are not nasty in any way. I remember a great scene before we were married when I said to Robert, 'I'd like to call your mother something.' He said, 'Go on, don't hold it back.' 'I can't,' I said, 'it would hurt you too much.' 'Go on you must,' he said. I said, 'I think she is a fat old cow.' He burst out laughing. I must say he has got slightly irritated of late when I tell him I think she is a fat old cow, which I do from time to time.

He gets on very well with my family although he finds family gatherings a bit wearing. My mother has come round to him and he adores her.

Before marriage I used to imagine that going to parties as a married woman would be quite different. There would be no more eyes across the room, no more looks, and envying other girls – but it all goes on just the same. I should be very miserable if men regarded marriage as a taboo. I am mainly monogamous because I am happily married and I want to stay with Robert, but I can't stop feeling interested in other men.

One of the points about him that used to irritate me when we first married was that he would never quarrel and hit back. As a child I was forever fighting, ding dong, ding dong. I could never get him to do this. I would bang on and on about something, really getting down to third-form level and in the end he would get seriously angry and storm off. We are not attuned on the quarrel level at all.

The essential practical difficulty of my life is having a baby son and no living-in help. I am ceaselessly organizing so I can go out for a break. During our holidays we leave him with my mother but last time we did I missed him dreadfully. It was no fun because my mind was on Paul. Yet the alternative – it's such a drag – baby-sitting in hotels and all that.

Robert regards him as an enjoyable luxury. He has no sense of responsibility about Paul's emotional life at all. He sees him as a little animal, to be played with, romped with and fed and put to bed. He enjoys him much more than he thought he would. But he feels no great tie as I do.

The problem of working is on my mind all the time. I think I probably have got a job now working in the mornings. It will mean leaving notes for the char and whizzing off and whizzing back to give my son his lunch so I don't know how it will work out. I do feel it is unfair educating women who are going to marry and produce baby sons and have no opportunity to use their education. Personally, I feel very guilty about it because I know that if I had a bit more energy and been less lazy I could have done a job ages ago. Lots of people I know have got around this problem very happily. You can rise above it.

Running a small flat is pretty good hell. You have to be absurdly tidy and clean. You can't leave clothes lying around anywhere. Organizing a household and planning meals is boring but I feel I do have a primitive duty towards my husband as he is earning a living.

When I'm depressed I feel that marriage is a dead end and here I am with a baby and a husband and what next and all my life I've thought of a horizon ahead and all we can do now is to have a few more children and buy a house. Then at other times I think it is absolutely marvellous being married. There is always someone to do things with. Robert would never suggest the unusual, but if I was to suggest, 'Let's climb Mount Everest', Robert would always say, 'Okay, I'll drive you there.' I never need go home from a party on my own. If I feel guilty, if I have hurt someone's feelings I have some-one to tell. We hate being apart, even for a night. I feel as if I am Patricia-and-Robert.

James and Suki

The Situation. A young couple from different family backgrounds attempt to come to terms with the basic problems of married life. Differences of attitude on sex and money are part of it. The couple have been married for six years and they have two children of four and nearly two.

The Husband. James, in his late twenties who comes from an established landed, county family. He is working his way through the family business and hopes eventually to succeed his father as chairman of the Board.

The Wife. In her mid-twenties. She is the daughter of an American university professor, a graduate in sociology and a left-winger in politics.

The Place. A modern, architect-designed house in Hampstead, London.

JAMES: We didn't start to sleep together thinking we are going to get married. It was more that we liked each other and enjoyed making love. Suki wrote to me from abroad telling me that she was pregnant and I had just finished some exams and I went to my father and he said, 'It's about Suki?' before I'd even opened my mouth and I said, 'Yes,' and he said, 'She's pregnant isn't she?' – I said 'Yes.' He said he expected it to happen sometime but it was a pity we couldn't have waited a bit longer, and we'd better get married. Apart from the fact that we wanted to get married anyway – he accepted the whole thing just like that. My mother was very upset. I am not sure what was the stronger reason – what the neigh-bours would think was one and the other that I had spoilt

Suki's life. She put the blame on me rather than her. It's taken three years for her to accept Suki as my wife.

SUKI: We had talked about marriage – but I felt that I was trapping James. I had immense support and love from both my parents. There was no question of an abortion in any of our minds – it just didn't occur to me, nor to my parents. Both of them said, 'If you don't want to marry James, don't feel you have to because of the baby.' My father wrote one of the nicest letters to James.

When I first knew I was pregnant James was taking his final exams and I didn't want to burden him with the news. In fact I became pregnant on almost the last night we spent together before I left. By the time I had it confirmed by a doctor, I had suspected it for long enough to become accustomed to the idea and so had my father, so that there was no great traumatic experience. The most difficult thing was writing to James for the next month and not mentioning it. The one thing I wanted to tell him I couldn't say until he passed his exams.

JAMES: I thought her letters indicated that she was cooling off.

SUKI: He comes from the wealthy, county shires. His father is chairman of a large combine group of companies. There are three children and they had always been brought up with lots of money – he's not silly about money but it's always been there. His mother I think wanted him to marry someone from the same sort of background. I admire her immensely but I will never be very close to her. James was always her favourite son. I am half American. I had been to university. I came from a left-wing intelligentsia background – all the things that were wrong by her standards. She controlled herself very well and although we've had a few blow-ups, is always good and kind to us. I like her as a person although I consider her narrow-minded. She has suffered in her marriage because the demands of being a company chairman's wife are very great. She was an artistic young girl and loved literature and poetry. Maybe some of her feelings for being against our marriage was that she felt I was in some way this sort of person and that I might have some of the same difficulties that she'd had.

James' father was always wonderful to me and county society as such accepted me very well. Because they felt that there had been some friction within the family, people went out of their way to be nice to me. I felt very much I was going to a foreign country.

JAMES: Marriage has made our relationship more solid. We depend on each other far more than we did, because we feel we are able to. Formerly we depended more on ourselves and were trying to impress each other. We are not trying to impress each other any longer. I should say that we love each other more but are considerably less 'in love', or infatuated may be a better word. And apart from loving each other, we are also friends.

SUKI: He's very mature. He's the rock – I'm the high-low person. I used to talk very knowledgeably about things I knew very little about. James is completely honest and stable and if he doesn't know something he says so. He sticks up for his point of view and doesn't say things unless he means them. He is the rock and this is what I need and what I wanted.

A lot of women try and compete with their husbands on the same level, whereas I feel that in a marriage somebody must be the head of the household. One person must have the final say – and this attitude has helped me. I don't think I have become a nonentity, which is what many of my contemporaries are afraid of. Wives often feel they will lose their own personality. I have my own opinions and I speak out, but in the last resort I feel that James must be the person who has the final say, otherwise nothing would ever really work in the administration of marriage.

As far as academic arguments are concerned, I stick to my views.

JAMES: I can't think of anything that we have had an

outright irreconcilable argument about. We both get to the stage where we find we are disagreeing violently and then we agree to differ. We both have our own opinions. But in certain areas I normally take the decisions.

SUKI: We try and talk about our differences rather than getting frantically upset and argumentative. You can so easily say things which can never be wiped out however much loving-up you do afterwards. I could never forget a really moody and maybe true statement my husband has made about me.

I'm twenty-seven and before marriage I always earned my own money. This is one of the few changes in my life I would welcome. I've brought no money into the marriage and I think it would make an enormous difference to my mental state if I had even £100 a year of my own and that James' Christmas presents didn't come out of my housekeeping saved up. This is the sort of thing that irritates me – I would so love to be able to give something to him out of my own savings.

JAMES: It doesn't make that much difference to me. Does it really matter whether the money comes out of the housekeeping allowance which I pay or out of a personal allowance I give her? In addition, a regular allowance would be a definite commitment which at this stage I feel I can't afford. I know she has this thing about wanting money of her own, but I don't understand it. She knows she has only to ask for what she wants within reason – and she is a most reasonable girl – to be given the money.

SUKI: Basically I am a domesticated person – some people loathe every minute of housework and would honestly prefer to see their children for about an hour a day. Maybe it's because I don't have to do it all all the time that I enjoy the amount that I do. I get a sense of satisfaction out of keeping the house nice. Jamie has very high standards and he always notices everything that is done. He always says, 'That's a lovely meal', or 'We haven't had that for dinner before', or

'Isn't that a new dress?' so that I feel like making an effort.

I spend one day a week in town – my day off. I go in with a girl friend and we usually go to one museum or one art gallery and then have lunch with some friends and we shop or we gossip. I have one complete break a week which makes an enormous difference. I get my hair done and until Christmas-time I was doing one afternoon a week voluntary work but I can't cope with that any more because Justin has so many invitations out to tea and so many of his friends come here and I don't feel I can leave all that sort of thing to the au pair alone.

James takes an enormous amount of trouble with the children, as we both feel that family life is very important. He is dotty about his son, like a lot of fathers these days. He always helps me to put the children to bed and if I'm particularly exhausted or tired or ill he will do the whole job. We try and devote at least one day at the weekend to the children in some form or other.

Because of the children we try not to be away together for a long time during the day on either Saturday or Sunday but we do get away for a whole weekend – perhaps once in two months. We normally go with the children, as I feel quite strongly that you cannot hope for children to become civilized, communicating people if they never participate in adult everyday activities, and if they are always left behind with the mother's help or au pair girl.

We have talked about it and I have decided that for many years I won't be able to take a job that takes up more than a couple of afternoons a week. I would hate to become a vegetable but I think this is a condition I can avoid. You can't rely exclusively on mental stimulation from outside. You need a certain amount of discipline within yourself to read, and not just trash and detective stories which I am inclined to do.

If I didn't have children I would do full-time social work as I have a good degree, but I don't regret giving up work. I know I cannot do two jobs properly. I'm not really so concerned about running the house on oiled wheels because if I had a full-time job I would get staff to help run the house, but I don't feel that somebody else should bring up my children.

JAMES: Children strengthen the bond between you but I believe you have to be very careful about not allowing the children to take your life over or the house over. I must say that there are times, on a Sunday morning, for example, when they trot into our bedroom when I want to make love to Suki and it's impossible.

SUKI: These are small irritations, but we have tried to be as careful as we can that they don't interfere too much. We do try to keep the house free of total chaos. Except on occasions, the children don't play in the sitting-room and they don't play in the dining-room. They have the nursery and the breakfast-room and they can make these as messy as they want. And they have the garden. They must be able to make a mess and do what they want but there must also be some places in the house where they know they cannot go wild.

JAMES: I think our happiest moments are the times when we manage to be alone together, to go out somewhere together, but not necessarily to go to bed. These are times when neither Suki nor I are tired and it might be a weekend or it might be an evening.

SUKI: I like sitting and talking to him and being completely relaxed without worrying about the children. It is these times when we are relaxed and basically alone that everything feels in harmony. James has my undivided attention, unless I am reading, which infuriates him.

We go up to James' parents' place on weekends quite frequently. I couldn't stay there for any length of time, but nor could James I think. We both feel that it is possible to make a compromise in the business of the conflicting demands of work and family life. We have talked a great deal about James' future as chairman. We both feel that a compromise is essential – he need not take on all the extra-curricular activities that his father has shouldered – and that you can still do your job very well and preserve some of your home and family life. He's the only one of the children to go into the family business and it's been especially difficult for him in the firm because he's got the boss's name and he's had to work twice as hard to prove himself. He's extremely good at it and loves it. Obviously he wants to get ahead but we don't feel that his being chairman is the only goal in life.

JAMES: We talk over everything and we do discuss our sex life more in general terms than most people do, I think. I want to make love more frequently than Suki does. I haven't yet sorted out in my mind whether it is something my body wants or something that my mind thinks my body wants.

SUKI: When you are having an affair and not living together geographically – you are just sleeping together – one takes every opportunity to make love. Whereas when you have the opportunity to sleep together every night, there is not the same urgency. It is something we have thought about quite consciously because it worried me – I wondered whether there was something wrong with me because I remember this time before we were married when we would hop into bed whenever we could. But why, if I am feeling tired, make a thing of it? I don't feel less sexy than I was before marriage. We have gone through the whole gambit of contraceptive devices. We started off with a sheath and after we were married we had a diaphragm, then I went on to the pill and now on the loop. James says he has noticed a relaxation on my part during each change of method. Even with the pill I had to remember to take it every day and I was always terrified in case I had forgotten to take it. Also I gained weight.

JAMES: The loop, I think, is by far the best if it fits. Nothing else is required to be done. Suki is now more relaxed about her love making. She makes love more when she feels she wants to rather than when the mere opportunity is there.

It is possible that if I was sent away for three months I might have a sexual relationship with a girl and I think Suki would understand it but wouldn't want to know about it. Equally it could happen that whilst I was away, she would want someone else to make love with. It is more unlikely, but possible.

SUKI: No, I would not want to know. Anyway I would assume before he went away that this would happen. If the relationship became serious I can't visualize the traditional scene discovering that my husband has been unfaithful and saying, 'I want a divorce immediately.' I think my own immediate reaction would be, 'Where have I gone wrong?'

JAMES: You don't have to get bored making love to the same person. Of the two possibilities – different partners and different methods with the same partner – I feel that the latter is more of a challenge.

SUKI: I think the vitally important thing is being able to talk about it afterwards. Also I think the most important thing is not to be worried if you don't achieve an orgasm. If you worry about it, it certainly won't happen.

JAMES: For me sex is a question of mood – what mood I am in when I make love will depend entirely on how I make love. But I am never satisfied until Suki has an orgasm. Not for unselfish reasons but because I often want to make love and she doesn't necessarily want to. Then there are times when she wants to make love and the normal methods do not work for her.

SUKI: I lie there sometimes when it is just pleasant to make love without necessarily having an orgasm. The closeness is enough. There are all kinds of sex styles within one relationship – taking sex, giving sex, exciting sex, grumpy sex, experimental sex, therapeutic sex, bored sex, cuddly sex.

James always tells me about the pretty girls he has seen on the way to work. Oddly enough I am delighted by it as I feel so proud and secure. James did the cleverest thing when a young, ex-boy friend of mine came back and talked to me a great deal when James was abroad. He fancied the position of being a young man in love with an older married woman and I was rather chuffed by it. And it did an enormous amount for my morale and instead of James playing the heavy-handed husband when he returned, he was sympathetic and understanding. The relationship died a very quick and natural death, instead of anything happening. I was sexually titillated because it was very nice to have someone become excited about me at the stage when I'd just had a baby and when I felt I had lost all my attractiveness.

JAMES: It was a very conscious act. I was exceedingly jealous. It was possible that she might have slept with him, although I was pretty sure that she would have been dissatisfied anyway and therefore would have come back on this score alone. I am sure I would have known that she had been with him even if she hadn't admitted it.

SUKI: The main thing I would find about having an affair with someone is that I would be so disillusioned if it didn't work sexually. We've been so lucky and our problems are minor ones and I can't imagine wanting to be bothered to go through with anyone to finally reach a satisfactory sexual relationship.

JAMES: There are times when I feel very guilty when I want to make love and Suki doesn't.

SUKI: Then I feel guilty because I feel I should want to.

Bill and Betty

The Situation. A middle-class marriage characterized by the traditional differences of interest and outlook between men and women. The couple have been married for eighteen years, and have two children.

The Husband. Bill, in his early fifties, a manager of a small engineering works in the North.

The Wife. Betty, in her mid-forties. Before her marriage she worked as a private secretary to the manager of a bank.

The Place. A semi-detached house built in the thirties in a residential housing estate on the outskirts of Leeds.

BETTY: I used to find being on my own at home a great trial when the children went to school. It isn't that I can't live with myself, and it isn't that I don't enjoy my home. I do. But I enjoy people much more. So five years ago I went to the inaugural meeting of a local branch of a women's club and as I banged the front door, Bill shouted out, 'Don't get too involved.' Rather funny. In the end I was pushed into being chairman and have been ever since.

He thinks my club women are rather chit-chat sort of people. But he does know how important they are to me in that I feel I am helping other people.

BILL: I do get tired of hearing all about the disagreements between her lady friends or of who is getting a bit spiteful.

One difference between us is that Bett likes meeting people, and I like meeting certain people. She doesn't mind where we go, if somebody asks us out she would accept without a quibble. I would be inclined to say, 'Oh, the So-and-so's, they're a bit heavy.' I'm more that way inclined, though there are occasions when I've said I'm not keen and I've gone along and quite enjoyed myself.

BETTY: He does enjoy what I call *male male* company. One evening not so long ago Bill took me out for a drink, and it doesn't happen very often because of his hours. It was supposed to be my treat and we went out with a friend of his, and his wife who is a scream. We went off to this nice local pub. Gwen and I sat at a little table at the back chatting away to ourselves.

Halfway through the evening, Gwen said, 'Look at those two at the bar chatting away to themselves. They have taken us out and they are deep in football, boxing and work.' They did remember to bring us a drink on one or two occasions.

BILL: I follow every sport. In the winter it's soccer, and in the summer it is tennis and cricket. I have played football in my day, I watched football when I was a teenager and so I know every trick of the trade and I go to see the game performed as other people go to the ballet or opera. Every Saturday I like to go off and watch a game and my elder boy, he's grown up to like it as well. Sometimes we travel a fair distance, sometimes it's only local. But Bett keeps on getting on to me about 'you and your football' sort of business.

In the summer when there is no football I've sat and watched television and she has appeared at about four o'clock in the afternoon with a cup of tea. I have said, 'I can't think why you miss me on a Saturday at football. This is the first time I've seen you for two hours.'

BETTY: I don't mind them going off every Saturday. But sometimes it is the way in which it is done that upsets me. When they go, it means I have to have lunch ready by twelve o'clock sharp so they have plenty of time to go trotting off to wherever the game is. Perhaps I have to get my washing done and out as well so it is quite a feat to keep to schedule.

Then I'm left with all the clearing-up, which I accept. But often it is three o'clock before I have a moment to call my own. Then he comes tearing in with three or four friends as well. Tea has to be on the table at five o'clock, sandwiches and the lot. He eats his tea quickly and goes off to work.

Saturday after Saturday after Saturday like this; you do get a bit scratchy.

I would go with them but honestly I would be in the way. He takes our boy, who is no small child, his friend and his friend's son. By that time the car is full. When I get to the game, unless I'm careful I can't see a thing except the man in front of me, as I'm so short. Bill is over six foot and so are the other men in the party. So it would mean looking round their knees. There's Mum!

BILL: After last year, I said I'm going on holiday on my own or I'm taking the boys on my own.

We had an awful lot of fuss and preparation getting away in the first place. When we got there either one boy was fed up because he wanted to go off roller-skating, and the other one was fed up because he wanted to go for a swim and nobody else wanted to go in, and Bett was fed up because there was nothing to do in the evenings, and I was fed up because I didn't want to be dragged off here there and everywhere and always doing something else.

Bett is not overkeen on swimming because she is afraid someone sitting on the sand will say, 'Look at that plump woman going in the water', which is a lot of nonsense. She is not keen on playing games like cricket, or she will play for quarter of an hour and then she's had enough.

I'd rather rough it a bit on holiday, take it easy and I wouldn't mind doing a bit of camping.

BETTY: His idea of a rest is a six-mile hike before breakfast. I enjoy walking but not always at the pace at which he wants to go. He has covered a mile when I'm only half way up the road.

He goes in for everything with much enthusiasm. At the holiday camp, he played football and ricked his ankle rather badly but fortunately I am a car driver so I was able to take us all out. A few days later he hurt his wrist playing cricket, and I had to do all the driving for the rest of the time.

We have never been abroad together on a holiday – Bill just won't go. I'm hoping he might change his mind but I think he saw enough of France and Belgium and Germany in the last war.

BILL: At home she gets lonely and fed up in the evenings and throws it in my face. That other people go visiting and she can't, and she can't ask people here because I'm at work. She grumbles a lot when I work overtime, but I have to point out to her, you can't have it both ways, you can't keep having time off and expect to earn more money.

BETTY: We are pretty equal really, our basic needs are the same or similar. He is a very kind person and fills up where I fall down.

I'd had the flu and felt pretty groggy and some minor mishap had occurred before the flu and I was very low indeed. The moment I could get up and go outside he bought me a new skirt which raised my morale no end. We went down to the shops on the Tuesday and I ensconced him in a chair and went off to pick out two or three skirts which I thought we would both like. Then I had a little mannequin parade of my own.

BILL: Betty always does look nicely dressed. We always look at some of our neighbours and say, 'Fancy going down the road looking like that.' But Betty wouldn't, she would have to dress up – just to fetch a tin of beans.

She has a dig at me sometimes, 'How are your girl friends at work?' and if I turn round and be naïve and tell her that I'm not interested in the women there, she gets suspicious. So I always say, 'There's two of my favourites on tonight.'

BETTY: One of the things a partnership must agree on is that love-making should go on being important.

I think sometimes it's not a bad thing for a husband and wife to be away from each other for a while and then come back again. There's no need for love-making to become stale and familiar. You can make love differently, you can behave differently. It's surprising when you look back after you've been married a good many years how you change towards each other. You think back and realize that things are not what they were.

BILL: Bett is not like so many wives I can think of who repeat, 'Yes, dear, no.' And they are not really listening, and they don't know what you are talking about. Her point of view is always worth hearing.

My sister-in-law for example, she never stops talking when she comes to our house. I can stand about fifteen minutes of her and I have to go out. On and on she goes and it's pure rubbish.

Bett is a good mixer, and when we go out and I meet one or two men she enters into the conversation equally as much as I have. But she's not bossy with it.

BETTY: If I felt very strongly about acting on an issue and disagreed with Bill I don't think I would go ahead and do it. I need his half-hearted approval even to start.

Of course, we have our moments, don't we all? He can be utterly selfish as far as I'm concerned.

The last straw for me was when I went to our National Conference this year. He has been marvellous in the past in that he hasn't minded me going at all for the three days. Though if he did mind I wouldn't go because that wouldn't be fair.

This particular time we planned on the Wednesday he was going to take the boys to Burnham Beeches for the day and come back, as I thought. And in the end he didn't come back. He borrowed a tent from a friend and he and the boys camped out in the woods while I was away. He had been planning this, he must have done, for about a fortnight beforehand because he had borrowed the tent and not said a word about it. And he had also told the boys not to say anything to me.

It was this that hurt so much. The thought that he did it without consulting me at all, I felt dreadful about it.

If he had of told me I would probably have said, 'Be careful and make sure you have this that and the other.' A woman always does fuss about pyjamas and the damp.

He isn't sorry. And this is why I wouldn't have it out with him afterwards. I would have become terribly upset again and I knew I wouldn't get anywhere.

7. Togetherness and Separation

Lord and Lady Longford

The Situation. A long-lasting marriage in which both husband and wife have combined a full family life and separate careers of their own in the public eye. Both husband and wife are Roman Catholic converts. They have been married for thirty-seven years and they have eight children.

The Husband. Lord Longford, former Leader of the House of Lords.

The Wife. Lady Longford, a former Labour Party candidate, a lecturer and author. Her last book, a biography of Queen Victoria, was on the bestseller list in this country and in the United States.

The Place. The Longfords' family house, Bernhurst, in Sussex.

LORD LONGFORD: I think it would be very difficult to become bored with Elizabeth, no one else has ever been, so I think if I became bored with her it would be a tremendous reflection on me. I think that two people who are happily married develop so many things in common, so many memories, so many interests, so many friends that they really should have far more to talk about than any two other people. There are endless things to talk about in a serious way, quite apart from private jokes.

LADY LONGFORD: Although a sustained interest in one man may be interpreted by the young as a sign of limitation of personality, I literally do enjoy going to things with Frank more than with anyone else. Maybe he's exceptionally good company. Take for example some event that we are both interested in, like an election. I love discussing it – the possibilities and the events and the personalities – far more with him than with anyone else. It's more fun, more amusing.

Parties are different. If I'm at a party I would never talk to him unless I knew nobody else. I remember once we went to a wedding reception and neither of us knew a single person and we had to talk to each other the whole time and it was a terrible flop. We went away after ten minutes. At a party I would never stand beside him. But afterwards I like discussing everything with him. But something which isn't a party, like going to a film or a theatre, I love to do with him, because we know each other very well.

LORD LONGFORD: I know a good many public men whose marriages have failed simply because they've left their wives behind. It seems to be more often the wife who gets bored with a man in public life because she doesn't see him. He has a very good time and she is left at home. I do see a good many political marriages which either break up openly or are known to be on the rocks, just for this reason. But obviously there are politicians who are quite happily married.

I've not served abroad, I haven't been compelled to live in New York or Geneva. The biggest strain is when a husband is abroad a lot of the time. Taken as a whole I spend almost every night under the same roof as my wife. In the evening I am just longing to see her after all the distractions of the day and I have plenty to tell her if I have been involved in a political day. I think I might be rather more amusing than if I had spent the whole day at home in the flat.

LADY LONGFORD: He is a tremendously good companion. In the early days of our marriage he didn't come home and put his feet up and say, 'Thank God I'm away from work.' He would always talk about what had been happening at the office and the people there. And I would complain about what had been happening in the house and how ill (being pregnant) I felt and he would listen sympathetically or pretend to.

By now we've been married for getting on forty years. We both need to be married. We are very uxorious types. Neither of us likes being alone and not having a stable companion. I think that is partly due to inheritance on both sides of our families. On Frank's side, his brother and sisters have been happily married – no divorces – and his mother and father were very happily married. On my side of the family all my brothers and sisters are happily married. I think form does count a certain amount.

LORD LONGFORD: In my prayers I would always pray for my wife first and last in any prayer I ever make, even in a quick prayer in the middle of the day. So that in a sense an effort comes in. You mustn't be too easy going about it and assume that you are the lucky one. I can imagine two people, both agnostics, who are happily married, obviously there are a lot in that position. But if two people have real leanings towards religious belief or if one has, I should have said that this was all important. I think religion is all-important to life so I think that poor happy humanists are missing something marvellous. But I can well imagine a successful marriage if neither was interested in religion, but as soon as religion comes in at all it comes in everywhere. Two people who share a common faith are bound together by that and it's a tremendous source of interest and common inspiration and consolation when you are going through a period of distress. But beyond that I'm happy to believe that religion does supply a firmness of character which Marxism and humanist doctrine wouldn't.

LADY LONGFORD: I don't think religion is of absolute importance in marriage but I think if it's there, it's important. In our own case, we were married in 1931 and Frank came into the Church in 1940, so that was nine years of marriage. Me without any religion at all and as far as I knew, Frank with an absolute minimum, but I didn't know he was secretly approaching the Church and it was a very unpleasant surprise to me when he came in. Then after six years I came in in 1946, by slow stages via the Anglican Church. Once you have religion I think it is a binding, common experience, but I didn't feel our marriage was in the slightest danger in the ten or twelve years when there wasn't any noticeable religion. Supposing Frank had never met Father d'Arcey, never had his Irish connexions which certainly helped to give him an interest in Catholicism, I still think our marriage would have been perfectly safe and sound. He might not agree but that's what I think. I also think our marriage would have remained perfectly safe and sound if he had gone into the church and I had remained outside. There were certain difficulties in those six years, when he was in the church and very, very enthusiastic. I don't mean that he isn't now but a new convert always has a special explorer's attitude. It was very intense and so although for the first few years I had been completely indifferent, I became anti for a year or two. We did have great arguments but I wouldn't say it had the slightest effect on our marriage. It never occurred to me or to him that our marriage was going to break up, or even be in difficulties.

All human relations are on a number of different levels. On the cerebral level, we certainly had tremendous arguments and complete difference of opinion. But the very fact that I did come in in six years must have meant that on another level there was something happening. You've got to have a seed stirring somewhere for it to happen at all. So presumably where there appeared to be on a cerebral level complete difference, at a deeper point, there probably was some unity, some agreement, which I wasn't aware of. I believe if the Archangel Gabriel had suddenly descended and said you've got to tell the absolute truth, are you really, utterly hostile, I would have jumped backwards with horror and said, don't ask!

LORD LONGFORD: I never think about our marriage at all. It's rather like asking myself how do I manage to breathe or how do you get off to sleep? If one sleeps badly one begins to worry about pills. Perhaps if I thought about it more, I would damage it. I would say that being in love from the beginning sustains my marriage. Once you are in love and you have a wife who has many interests in common with you, it would seem to me that the relationship wouldn't need further stimulation. I would think it odd if real love faded unless it was mainly sexual. I think there ought to be a strong sexual element, if that is not present, you might get a couple who got on very well together without much sexual attraction. Without sexual attraction the marriage would be incomplete. But a relationship mainly based on sex would probably fade as people got older and sex began to play a less prominent part in their life, and you might wish you had married a fellow-artist or a doctor if you are a doctor. It would then be too late to wish for a wife with similar interests when your marriage was based on sex. But where you've got the sexual attraction and the common interest, then all should be well.

I don't want to make it sound too perfect.

LADY LONGFORD: The old phrase about common interests is a true one. I think you need a certain number of these though you can have some fringe interests which may be very important to you which aren't shared. The marriage spectrum has got to have some colours in common but you can have some each end which don't overlap. For instance, Frank is mad keen on sport and I'm not the slightest bit. I'm interested in flowers and birds and the house and all the rest of it and he isn't. But I suppose those are really male and female specialities which we each have. We don't share here. But all the intermediate, what I would call human interests, like books and politics and drama and people and gossip, we both share, and the children naturally.

I think the most dangerous years really are the first ten years. Your husband hasn't become a habit in the sense of being an essential part of your life. He hasn't had time to. You're presumably rather young, you're still aware of other people, you need your old friends from your pre-married days, you're still meeting them and there is an emotional relationship with them. I think you could perfectly well have various affairs at the same time thinking your marriage is your basic one, and

then to your surprise you may find one of the affairs outside
has suddenly eclipsed your marriage, after you've been married
about six or seven years. I think that can happen and I think
it would happen but for one thing – a marriage has got to be
going forward and strengthening all the time. I do not see
how that can develop unless you have long periods together
when you really are isolated. By that I mean two or three
evenings a week not going out. If I hear that young married
couples go out every evening, even if they go out together,
even if they start out together and come home together, I
always think this is going to be dangerous.

We were very lucky in a way because when we married we
lived in the country at an awful place to get to, and there was
nowhere to go out. Coming home Frank was always late, so
we met with a row, me in an absolute fury, especially if I was
pregnant, but having got over that we did have the evening
together. So our marriage went forward.

LORD LONGFORD: I've been lucky. There are parents who
don't like their children. But I've always liked them all. I've
got more interested in them as they've got older. I'm not keen
on babies, I don't mind the squeaking but I can't tell one from
another.

Now the children are less with us and we are in our London
flat without any children. At weekends they come and go. The
one time when they are rather overpowering is at Christmas –
it would be difficult to stand up to that. I usually retire to bed
most of the time. There are such a lot of them, and grand-
children. A bit formidable.

LADY LONGFORD: There was a time when we did talk
more about our children and their problems than any other
subject. Now we talk about other things nearly as much. We
very much enjoyed the children, we wouldn't have had so
many if we hadn't. The only time we both felt that they
intruded was when the first batch grew into their teens and
were not yet independent. They were still living at home but

would stay up for dinner with us, and in fact were there from dawn till bedtime. We did realize that it is the human cycle and you have to adapt yourself but this is a great shock to a lot of parents who are always used to the children being a delightful daytime event, which disappears at about seven o'clock.

I was very fascinated to find that Queen Victoria and Prince Albert, who were absolutely devoted to each other, found this a trial. When their eldest daughter, Vickie, began staying up for meals, at first she thought how marvellous, she really is growing up, how lovely, and began thinking of a nice German prince for her to marry. And then, how horrid this is, she is always there. Then she got married very early and then here were the others coming along and they never got back to the peaceful, private time.

When the children are there at all meals talking the whole time, you don't get any separate conversation. I just said thank God for television which was in a different room and they did take themselves off after dinner. But if they'd grown up in the days before television and there'd been only one sitting-room, then I would have had to retire to my bedroom for privacy.

LORD LONGFORD: I'm entirely against premarital sex and cannot see any advantage in the trial spin idea. I think it is disgusting. The only advantage is if people are not going to get married and they need sex as an outlet, it might have a mildly therapeutic effect, but in the long run they'll pay for it. Young people may say that if you marry someone without sleeping together it's just possible you might have picked a sadist. You must know if the man's a sadist or not without going to bed with him.

My generation was obsessed with sex. They talked of nothing else but D. H. Lawrence if they were at all intellectual. I don't think any writer has dominated the present generation as much as Lawrence did mine. Not that I was interested in Lawrence but my wife was. I would say that my era was absolutely dominated by sex and men were much more homosexual – I'm talking about the professional or intellectual classes – than they are today. I think the great change is that girls enter into the lives of men – again I'm talking about the professional classes – very much earlier than they did before. I never met an undergraduette until I met my wife on the last day of my last term at Oxford.

I think that young people do sleep together more outside of marriage now than they did then, because illegitimacy has gone up. But even there I took part in an Oxford debate on the subject of premarital chastity two or three years ago and the Christian side, the chastity side, won overwhelmingly. So people talk about it more than they do it. Or they don't vote for it. I should have thought that sex had dominated the thoughts of young people always.

LADY LONGFORD: I've always luckily had a career, a semi-career, that was compatible with children. I didn't give it up immediately I married because I was lecturing for the WEA and that was compatible with married life. I stopped just when Antonia was very much on the way and then I started again and then did another WEA course and then Thomas was on the way and I gave it up again and then I started some more and then I stopped that and then started nursing a constituency – and in fact stood in an election. Thomas was a year old – I stood for Cheltenham in 1935. I stood but it was a hopeless seat. I fought the election and then retired. Then for the next seven years I nursed a seat in Birmingham, taking Paddy with me and leaving him in his carry-cot at the back of the hall. He slept through the applause as it was not directed at him. It was tremendously strenuous because the war started just after Paddy was born and finally I had to give up my Birmingham constituency because of the difficulties driving to and fro. There was the petrol shortage and every other known domestic problem and leaving the children. Although I didn't ever have to leave them for a night, it was difficult. I had a long period from about 1943 to 1950 with no career of any sort. Frank got into the government meanwhile, so I had all the fun of being a political wife which was a new thing. I suppose that filled many gaps. And then when my youngest was about three, by chance I began doing journalism for the *Daily Express* which was tremendously lucky.

I sometimes have asked myself whether I regretted giving up active political life. I could certainly have got into Parliament because the last seat that I nursed for seven years had a 12,000 majority when the '45 election came, so I would have been in a safe seat. But, no, because I think it would have been incompatible with our family lives, as Frank didn't get in in '45. If we'd both been in, it would have been great fun. But now I've gone off on a different tack of writing history and I love that. I've reached the age when anyway I might be finding a constituency rather a strain.

LORD LONGFORD: I'm not at all good at holidays. The idea of holidays is one I've never run to. When I have what is called a holiday I like to think I'm making use of it – writing a book or at least writing a long article or trying to learn some new elderly sport. We have a small house in Sussex and we have holidays there. I'm never good at going away for a long time, I'm not a person who's ready to go for a cruise for three weeks or go to Scotland for a month.

LADY LONGFORD: Frank doesn't like holidays at all lasting more than forty-eight hours. He used to hate going abroad, although he's more tolerant now. I would never dream of taking him on a trip to Spain for instance. He would have liked to have seen the battlefield of Salamanca, because his ancestor did very well there, but he would have taken the next plane home. I garden during the holidays at home.

If you live surrounded by earth you've got to do something with it. A dull garden is one of the most depressing spectacles. So taking the pure necessity of doing something with the ground that surrounds you, you make a start. Then finally you get swept away by catalogues and other people's gardens. A garden is part of the home, an outdoor extension of what one does in one's sitting-room.

LORD LONGFORD: We are active comrades. In the election we did tours together and when we lived in Oxford we did work together. Now Elizabeth's main intellectual activity is writing, her creative book-writing and mine is that of a politician. In a sense they are separate lives but we can both help each other. It is not like a couple in Parliament who are both ministers or when the wife is an assistant to the husband. Elizabeth has control of the house and her own creative work and I have politics and other social activities, but bound together by marriage and living together. From Friday to Monday we shall be together and no children coming at all so we really see each other a lot. Minor difficulties arise when I feel I ought to make a speech on a Friday. I always try to think of her when I make these decisions and if possible get her to agree. If a man thinks, 'My profession comes first', then in the end it can destroy his marriage – equally he must make his wife realize that he ought to be doing other things, otherwise he wrecks his career. He has got to think of both and in the end I would always put my marriage first. I would like to say that my marriage was successful but I don't want to be in the position of boasting about it.

LADY LONGFORD: Whatever you do during the day you need each other's company in the evening, some evenings a week, as a regular thing. Now we're both so busy that very often there hardly does seem an evening alone together, but at the weekend we get to Bernhurst. We practically always have Friday evenings, and I always make a fuss if several Fridays running Frank doesn't come down because of engagements.

Now I'm religious in a feeble sort of way I do think of my latter days. You naturally do. When you're three score years you say, ten more years? fifteen more years? Then you think the same about your husband, you feel he's even more precious and important because you may not have each other for all that long. You certainly don't think, 'Are you bored?' Absolutely the opposite. You think of making the most of what's left.

Peter and Jane

The Situation. A marriage in which physical separation is the general state and togetherness is occasional. Since the beginning of the marriage eleven years ago, the husband's work has involved him in extensive travel away from home. The couple have five children, aged nine months, nearly two, three plus, eight and ten years.

The Husband. Peter, aged thirty-three, an Oxbridge graduate, is an executive employed by an oil company. He married at the age of twenty-two.

The Wife. Jane, aged thirty, an art-school graduate.

The Place. A large detached house with a garden, built in the 1930s in the green belt.

PETER: When we married we both realized that we were at the beginning of life and we wanted to build our lives together. Living together would have been better than nothing, but as a relationship we felt it wasn't nearly enough. But as we have grown up we have both discovered that we are completely different human beings – to a degree that we never suspected when we fell in love. This happens of course in every marriage.

Jane dislikes public life. I think she thinks, and sometimes I agree with her, that people involve themselves in public life because of personal insufficiency. In some ways she is anti-life. To me involvement in my work, involvement for the sake of it, is an inescapable part of life.

I have made attempts during different periods to try to persuade myself that I am self-sufficient within the home and a nine-till-five job. Invariably, the experience produces a deep psychological reaction and I can only recover from this by flinging myself right back into the maelstrom.

JANE: The first few years required an almost impossibly painful adjustment, especially because I was on my own such a great deal. Peter first went away when I was three months pregnant – that wasn't too bad because we were going through a bad patch and it came as a relief, almost.

I was in a basement flat in Paddington, pregnant and weepy – not a good start. Our marriage was far worse when Peter was at home than when he went away. I was feeling sick and ill, and he can't bear me being pregnant. He goes off me completely. The physical side was a total failure and if he can't have plenty of sex he can't work. So our life is an absolute misery through every pregnancy. Now I can understand it and accept it but then I was still discovering what marriage is about. I thought the end of the world had come. All I knew was we were married, I was having a baby, and bang! – all affection went.

Peter was too young to understand how he felt. He just knew I was miserable with him, miserable without him; there seemed no way in which I could make him happy. I told a doctor friend that I wanted to put my head in a gas oven and she told me how ridiculous and unnecessary and gave me some pills. That did make things a bit better. I told Peter that many men suffered from the causes that distressed him and that he was not alone. I think he thought it was only me, and my God! what *had* he chosen in the way of a wife? Some awful creature who goes around moping after babies and would never be normal again.

PETER: There have been dangerous periods when I am away. Small, intimate, important details go wrong and you can't count on the time needed to try to set matters right or to remedy misunderstandings. A case in point. I had been working in Kuwait for four months and hadn't seen Jane or the children for nearly five months. I managed to wangle an air fare for her. She arrived totally exhausted by a bad night on the plane. A few hours after her arrival I got a telegram ordering me away the very next day.

Now our relationship depended on that one night, and it is a very fragile link, one night with a tired girl. We had an agonizing three months afterwards because we both knew that things were not right.

JANE: One assumes that your body is going to react in the advertised way and that everything is going to be perfect, but it's not. I think that the physical side of a relationship takes a long time to develop with some people. Certainly this is true for us, and when we reunite after being apart for months, we have to start almost from the beginning.

On that occasion I was a fool to go in any case. I could hardly speak at all, I was so exhausted after the trip. I felt guilty about leaving the new baby behind with my mother – and I looked ghastly, bulgy, with lank hair. Peter, whom I hadn't seen for five months, was in top form, gay, lively and longing. I broke down, and became weak and mimsey, so then Peter said if you do not pull yourself together I shall DIVORCE you. It was the last straw, this feeling so helpless and hopeless. I pulled through in the end. You never forget threats, the person who says them may, but the receiver – never.

When he breezed back for a day or two or a month perhaps it used to be difficult for both of us. I am rather regular in my life and a very tidy sort of person. Peter is appallingly untidy and so the house is a shambles within five minutes of his return. Little things like that used to irritate me but not any more. Now I don't expect things to be as they were, *ever*, when Peter returns.

I never ask him what he has done or who he has met – I listen when he volunteers information. No one wants to come home to an interrogation. Home must always be a haven whatever you have done or however long you have been away and as for questions about anything that betrayed our trust in each other ... well I don't believe in having complete trust. Peter thinks I should but I think that's very dangerous.

PETER: If Jane had affairs with other men it would have destroyed the marriage. I am not saying that I demand implacable fidelity in every way but you can be unlonely without rolling in bed with people. I do think that men have different physical needs to most women. I think it is much easier for men to have fleeting sexual relationships on occasion without a significant sense of disloyalty and without any real betrayal, than it is for most women. This may be and I dare say is a hideous male rationalization.

JANE: I expect some day he will go off, as the temptations are almost irresistible. Two people like us in a continual state of development throughout their married lives might easily start drifting even farther apart. I am much less intellectual than Peter and possibly more creative, but our fields of interest do not overlap and this is another source of friction.

I'm a terrific worrier. I worry psychopathically about these things, and if I allowed my mind to dwell on it I would be an emotional wreck. The worry is torture. But I would much rather suspect than have my suspicions confirmed.

I paint in my own studio and I work in a local Family Planning Clinic. But there have been long periods when I have not been able to fit in any work of my own outside the family. When the children are ill or I'm having a baby it is very difficult to keep up the standards I like to keep up at home and give anything of value to my own work. So that's the great danger; as the woman in the house, you become a bore. Nothing is drearier than domestic routine especially if you are tired all the time.

PETER: When I am away I do respect Jane's judgement in regard to the home and the children, although I constantly pitch out advice which is very often followed.

One extraordinary thing is that I believe there are few fathers that I have met that know their children as well as I know mine. And I have spent a long long time away from home. There is constant excitement in our relationship. It's not an artificial thing. But I am immensely close to them and I am sure they feel it very much.

Besides, distances are not what they were. I can be in the Middle East at eleven, at London Airport at three p.m. and picking them up from the village school at four. They write, they are obliged to put their thoughts on paper to tell me about themselves. When you are away small things mean more. You can come back from the office and say, 'Good-night, darling. Daddy loves you very much.' But if you say it in a telegram from Saudi Arabia they do believe it. Another factor is that they are never quite sure when I will be home, as I am not sure myself. So they don't expel all thought of me from their minds. Jane is good too, in that she doesn't let my existence disappear in the house.

The sense of continuity at home is vital to the success of the whole thing for me. But Jane's natural independence of mind is very valuable too. She has her own artistic interests and her welfare work. If she was wholly dependent on me for her stimulation or for succour our marriage would be much more vulnerable, and equally me.

JANE: My marriage has gone in phases – I think all marriages do. When my first two children were little I devoted myself to them entirely. At this stage I would have been faced with a very serious conflict of loyalties if Peter had thought it was more important for me to be free to travel with him. But I think that it is being up all night with little children, seeing them through their troubles and always being with them every day that gives them a sense of security. If you do take this trouble you are likely to be able to communicate with them all their lives.

In those days we led such separated lives that we began to find the marriage drifting and our meeting grounds fewer and fewer. I found that I wanted to involve myself in Peter's life more. Really, the marriage needed it. So we decided to employ an experienced nanny who is still with us, and I accepted opportunities to travel with Peter and go around with him. I have never believed in being a shadow, but I took more of a part in his life.

I suppose I am less close to the youngest children, but the fact that we are a large family makes everything more relaxed and unified. I am very close to the older children, whom I looked after myself, and this tends to set the pattern. The older children know that I am Mum and as a consequence, the little ones do too.

For me, marriage is a question of being able to find an individual life of my own to fit into the framework of the whole. I do find that these days the prison bars are opening.

When he goes away without me I get a slight pang, but I pack him off in a flurry and that's that. I pick up a different sort of life. I'm sorry he is not there to share it, but I don't pine. If you are to survive as a separate individual the key to this private identity must be found.

I personally am unable to reconcile having children with the career I had always hoped for. I do not see how you can have a home when the wife is not there most of the time. You can have a house that runs efficiently but I don't think you can have a home. Peter comes back from the office and from his trips absolutely whacked, flat out. I try to have a rest in the afternoon so that when he comes home I am in good form and ready to absorb his thoughts or to boost his morale or make him laugh and be himself again. If I did a real job of work outside the home I would need a booster myself, and I know when I am asking for the moon.

Eleanor

The Situation. An elderly professional couple have been married for over fifty years. The couple had two children, a daughter who is married and a son who was killed in the last war.

The Wife. Eleanor, in her early seventies. An Oxford graduate, she keeps up her lifelong interest in teaching and coaches candidates for university entrance. Her husband is in his ninetieth year and is a former civil servant.

ELEANOR: I nearly didn't marry him. I was watching him pack a suitcase one day. Little boxes for this and little envelopes for that. Far too pernickety and meticulous. I thought is this a sign of something else I won't be able to stand? We're too different.

It is extraordinary how much importance I attached to trivial incidents. But I have found him to be pernickety about minor points that don't matter and almost rashly adventurous about major issues – a trait I love.

We are temperamentally very different, almost opposite. His impulse is to shut away his difference of opinion behind cold anger and disapproval. Mine is to say probably a lot of unforgivable things and then forget them the next moment. If I can't burst out I feel terrible.

So much of my early fighting was basically to keep my end up – I feel my identity has now long been established.

I held a standard of perfectibility for him and fundamentally I would always rather prove myself wrong in a discussion because if I destroyed his case I minded that dreadfully. In my heart, I wanted him to be right.

Gradually, he taught me to respect another person's personality – with a husband of a less strong character I should probably have become a bully – and perhaps I taught him to be more sympathetic and patient. The rows, which were never frequent or lasting, have died out. The realization that we have mellowed is comforting, if a bit boring!

My husband won't let me look after him and I'm only too glad not to. I'm never allowed to do personal chores for him except cooking and washing-up. He sews on his own buttons, he won't allow me to touch a thread and he never even allows me to darn his socks, for which I am eternally grateful.

I am a bad housewife, I am not interested in it. I do occasional dusting. I don't like to see dirt but if it is not visible it doesn't worry me at all. I do mind very much about the look of a room and my husband and I differ about this, because I don't think he sees what a room is like unless you absolutely rub his nose in it. He wouldn't notice if there were any flowers or not. Left to himself, his room would be in a most unattractive state in a day. But he is tidy in himself and horribly tidy in his drawers. I am exactly the opposite – I don't mind what my drawers look like but I can't sit quietly in a room with the furniture all higgledy-piggledy and dead flowers.

Food is a necessary affliction because it has got to be done every day and if I could have one meal a week I should be really interested in preparing it. But it really makes me ill to think of how many meals I have eaten and washed-up when you get to my age. We were both brought up in a puritan nonconformist background and we share simple tastes. He doesn't in the least mind going on with cold meat and rice pudding every day if I felt inclined. My husband always gets the breakfast – we don't have a cooked breakfast. I reckon really to do cooking once a week and as little as possible otherwise.

Sometimes in the winter evenings I read out loud my old journals of our travels together. They were day-by-day jottings when we were in the East many years ago. We were there for six months. And then every time since we have been abroad I have kept a diary. Sometimes it is a chore but it's worth it because we do forget and as we get older we forget more. They are fascinating to read over and over again and share them. We take the diaries in cycles and look at our photographs.

We both keep our separate interests, very important. We should become dreadfully bored with each other if we had to share every single moment of the day. A friend of about my age has moved into a much smaller house as a lot of people of our group have had to, and she finds it a strain to have to share a sitting-room all the time with her husband, although she is happily married. She was used to doing her work in one room whilst he worked in another. Now they have just the one room which they spend all their time in. I don't think the husband minds at all but she has had to make the best of it.

I use the dining-room or kitchen or my bedroom, and my husband has his study.

I dislike things, except books perhaps. I don't want to accumulate things. I would like to finish my life in a cell, not having to bother about possessions any more. I would like to think I am becoming more spiritually-minded and less materialistic but it is probably that I can't be bothered with the dusting.

Sex was a major force in our marriage until he was well past eighty. I'm twenty years younger and could have gone on for longer but I do now get extremely tired at the end of the day and I have no regrets. My husband felt apologetic because of me being younger but there wasn't any real need. The process of fading out is gradual, you try and it doesn't work, you might try again and it does. There was a natural reluctance on both our parts to attempt what might prove a failure, so gradually sex faded out. When sex stops any time after eighty no man can feel that there is anything wanting in his virility. It stopped for purely physical reasons of advancing age.

With some men I should have been repressed, because I was brought up in what was the Victorian attitude towards sex. And therefore if my husband had not been a skilled and careful and ardent lover I might never have discovered the physical pleasures of love. What luck! We do occasionally discuss the ending of our sex life and we just say isn't it a pity and how enjoyable it would be if we were both fifteen years younger. But this isn't a problem, just a mild regret.

Some aspects of our marriage haven't changed. His sense of humour, my delight in the way he lightens up a situation is just as fresh. A wry and funny comment of his did the trick on the first evening we went out and has never failed me since.

When I go home in the evenings I always tell him everything that has happened to me during the day. He reads his newspaper and says 'um.' 'You're not listening,' I say. And he says 'um.' Then he does begin to listen.

Our greatest pleasures together remain the ones we have always shared – music, pictures, ideas, books, places. We are quite capable of holding an impassioned philosophic argument after breakfast when the washing-up is still to be done, and often do. The absolute basic foundation of our marriage is that we share the same values – this is tremendously important to us both.

Everyone has a physical shrinking from death and the unknown but I don't think it is death that I really fear. I dread senility. Lucky old people die suddenly. I have a horror of losing my personality, yet remaining physically alive. If this happens all the people you love most are going to long for your death. You are such a burden. If I could get hold of a safe reliable way of ending my life it would be a great comfort and I certainly believe that I would have the determination necessary to do it when the time came. You do get a warning and that is the time, your memory and your powers don't go suddenly – just like that.

I used to think that because of his seniority my husband would die first but now I am not so sure. It is he who looks after me at the moment. Nevertheless I keep on saying to myself that I must make provisions for being on my own, but I don't.

When you get to the stage of having lived together as much as we have it will be an awful blow. I don't think it is much good preparing for it. I think it will be almost impossible to share a home with anybody else after living with a husband for so long. I can't expect that there will be time to grow to adjust to somebody else.

I have a religious temperament and a sceptical mind. I have to live with myself and therefore, although the concept of life after death remains a hope, I have accepted the fact that I must live in uncertainty. But I possess a real hope, a hope rather than a faith and this makes all the difference to us both, for we agree about this.

I think about death. Ever since the death of my son I have felt as if a bit of me has died. I think of death increasingly not as something that happens to other people but as something that, thank goodness, will happen to oneself as well as to others.

This stage is the test of whether a marriage has been successful or not. You learn whether you have been using a career, or your children to bolster it up. On the other hand if it has been successful you have been moving through the years to a fuller knowledge of each other.

Endpiece

'What are your conclusions?' is a question I am frequently asked by people who have known about this book. My principal conclusion is that there are no rounded, global generalizations which wrap up the state of modern marriage. It seems to me that in marriage people speak for themselves alone. I find it encouraging that the marital tie remains the most personal, volatile and unclassifiable of human bonds. No marriage can be tidied away into definitive pigeon holes or completely explained away by neat sociological, economic or psychological labelling. Marriage, I am convinced, is going to be the last subject to be effectively computerized.

Human motivations and needs are often so subtle and devious that it becomes difficult to lay down any firm ideas on the qualities which make for lasting marriage. Think of a seemingly safe statement, and qualification rears its awkward head.

It might be imagined that personal happiness and contentment remain a common goal. For many people, yes. But some married couples thrive on conflict, abuse and violence. Marriage, it may be claimed, is basically the state of togetherness. But many are the marriages where partners prefer to remain free of the bonds of marriage within the context of matrimony – and the arrangement can work. The importance of money in marriage has long been recognized. But, given a minimal standard of living, I think it would be difficult to correlate successful marriage and money.

However, there are certain attributes of a good marriage

which seem unlikely to change. Mutual affection, tenderness, a tolerance of the other person's idiosyncrasies, a pleasurable sex life, and a sense of sharing are the lifeblood of lasting marriage. These may be judged as being simple home-truths, but perhaps it is part of the unchanging nature of men and women in marriage that they remain responsive to such basic human qualities.